"In *Making All Things New*, David Powlison offers us a gem, a helping hand, and a sure bet. True to the Bible, he is a realist. He shows us how a Christ-redefined life changes what sex means. This book is not pie in the sky. It is feet on the floor. Where do you or people you love struggle? Take David's hand and walk this road with the Lord. He shows us all how besetting sexual sin is symptomatic of something yet hidden. Repentance of sin commences sexual repatterning, and this accessible book will take you into that dark place with the light of Christ. As the world clamors about sexual rights and privileges, the people of God must show up with something beyond moral platitudes or behavioral modification programs. We already have a Savior who knows how to rescue his people. And now we have an accessible guidebook, one that helps the sexual sinner recognize the deeper battle, and one that helps parents and allies apply faith to the dire facts of being held captive."

Rosaria Butterfield, former professor of English, Syracuse University; author, *The Secret Thoughts of an Unlikely Convert*

"Sexual sin can seem like a trap from which one can never escape. David Powlison brings good news to those caught in sexual sin, and to those who have been sinned against. This book addresses sexual sin not with shame and moralizing but with the gospel of Jesus Christ. We all need to hear the message of this book."

Russell D. Moore, president, Ethics & Religious Liberty Commission of the Southern Baptist Convention

"David Powlison's ministry to all fallen humanity is evident in this book. He calls those impacted by the pain and sorrow of sexual struggle and sin to repentance while finding refuge in the arms of our faithful Savior. Likewise, he presents to all who bear God's image a picture of what God is doing to restore the beauty of sexual intimacy in the lives of his people."

Timothy Geiger, president, Harvest USA; author, *What to Do When Your Child Says, "I'm Gay"*

T0324280

"Finally, a gospel-centered book for both genders that beautifully brings the hope of Christ to bear upon broken sexuality. Women, like men, have been sinned against sexually and have pursued their own expressions of sinful sexual behavior. *Making All Things New* masterfully achieves the author's vision to be candid and hopeful regarding the real possibility of life transformation and restored joy to women and men bound up in the shame and pain of sexual brokenness."

Ellen Mary Dykas, women's ministry coordinator, Harvest USA; author, *Sexual Sanity for Women: Healing from Sexual and Relational Brokenness*

"I love David Powlison. Few living authors have shaped my approach to gospel growth, and even preaching, more than he has. Gifted Christian counselors like Powlison read the Bible in a unique way, laying open both the truth of Scripture and the foundations of the human heart, showing where one intersects the other. I have to think that if you heard Jesus preach in the first century, you would have assumed you were listening to a very gifted counselor. In this remarkably insightful book, Powlison offers gospel hope to those who have sinned through sex and those who have suffered through it. I am excited to provide this resource to people dealing with an area in which many first experience their need of the gospel."

J. D. Greear, pastor, The Summit Church, Raleigh-Durham, North Carolina; author, *Gaining by Losing: Why the Future Belongs to Churches That Send*

"*Making All Things New* is a helpful perspective for understanding a common theme in life. David Powlison will help you to see sexual transgression and sexual affliction under the unique lens of the gospel, and will guide you to find hope in the purity and the cleanness of Christ. Jesus makes all things new, even our sexual experience."

Alexandre Chiaradia Mendes, pastor, Maranatha Baptist Church, São José dos Campos, Brazil; director of vision and expansion, Brazilian Association of Biblical Counselors; coauthor, *Dating and Engagement That God Desires*

"Nothing hinders joy more than sexual misuse and abuse, and nothing troubles more people more profoundly today than sexual deception, corruption, and brokenness. This easy-to-read book is compassionate yet uncompromising, practical yet principled. It shines light into darkness for those seeking a way out, and extends hope to those needing it most desperately."

Daniel R. Heimbach, senior professor of Christian ethics, Southeastern Baptist Theological Seminary; author, *True Sexual Morality: Recovering Biblical Standards for a Culture in Crisis*

MAKING
ALL
THINGS
NEW

Restoring Joy to the Sexually Broken

DAVID POWLISON

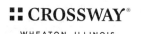

∷ CROSSWAY®

WHEATON, ILLINOIS

Some portions of this book appeared as David Powlison, "Making All Things New: Restoring Pure Joy to the Sexually Broken," chapter 4 in *Sex and the Supremacy of Christ*, ed. John Piper and Justin Taylor (Wheaton, IL: Crossway, 2005).

Cover design: Micah Lanier

Cover image: Quilt provided by Nan Powlison

First printing 2017

Printed in the United States of America

Unless otherwise indicated, Scripture quotations are from the ESV® Bible (The Holy Bible, English Standard Version®), copyright © 2001 by Crossway, a publishing ministry of Good News Publishers. Used by permission. All rights reserved.

Scripture quotations marked NASB are from *The New American Standard Bible®*. Copyright © The Lockman Foundation 1960, 1962, 1963, 1968, 1971, 1972, 1973, 1975, 1977, 1995. Used by permission.

Scripture references marked NIV are taken from The Holy Bible, New International Version®, NIV®. Copyright © 1973, 1978, 1984, 2011 by Biblica, Inc.™ Used by permission. All rights reserved worldwide.

Trade paperback ISBN: 978-1-4335-5614-2
ePub ISBN: 978-1-4335-5617-3
PDF ISBN: 978-1-4335-5615-9
Mobipocket ISBN: 978-1-4335-5616-6

Library of Congress Cataloging-in-Publication Data

Names: Powlison, David, 1949– author.
Title: Making all things new: restoring joy to the sexually broken / David Powlison.
Description: Wheaton: Crossway, 2017. | Includes bibliographical references and index.
Identifiers: LCCN 2016055822 (print) | LCCN 2017026211 (ebook) | ISBN 9781433556159 (pdf) | ISBN 9781433556166 (mobi) | ISBN 9781433556173 (epub) | ISBN 9781433556142 (tp)
Subjects: LCSH: Sex—Religious aspects—Christianity. | Consolation.
Classification: LCC BT708 (ebook) | LCC BT708 .P69 2017 (print) | DDC 261.8/357—dc23
LC record available at https://lccn.loc.gov/2016055822

Crossway is a publishing ministry of Good News Publishers.

BP		32	31	30	29	28	27	26	25	24
14	13	12	11	10	9	8	7	6	5	4	3

To Nan

CONTENTS

INTRODUCTION

A vibrant quilt has adorned a wall in our home for many years. The artist took bright swatches of fabric and cut hundreds of tiny squares and triangles. She created a lattice pattern through which you gaze into a luminous, iridescent garden. I view her quilt as an invitation to pause and catch a glimpse into a paradise. The latticework encloses, protects, provides structure, and reveals wonders. The garden within creates an impression of flower and color, air and light, life and pleasure. It gives a small picture of our God's two great works: the goodness of his creation and the goodness of his salvation.

Both creation and salvation embrace human sexuality. Sex is an elemental good in God's fruitful work in creation. Our sexuality is a renewed good by his fruitful working in salvation. Imagine sexuality transformed into a garden of wise love, safety, wisdom, self-control, and delight.

Imagine growing up within the protection of the lattice. Children are protected from the stains of betrayal, molestation, and assault. Sons and daughters are not defiled and sexualized by exposure to lewd humor and to suggestive or pornographic images. The sexually immature are cared for.

Imagine the dignity of sexual restraint as the first lesson of budding adulthood. We enter sexual maturity as singles, not marrieds. Friends, brothers, sisters, children, parents, and strangers are never meant to become objects of sexualized attention. Every willing learner must learn (and often relearn) broad-spectrum self-control as a core expression of love. And those who eventually marry will find that there are seasons where sexual restraint is the form love takes.

Imagine sexual desire freed and focused within the union of husband and wife. There is love, pleasure, and beauty in sexual expression during those seasons when it is a core facet of marital fidelity and love. Our sexuality was designed to be a willing servant of love. It becomes distorted by our willfulness or our fear. It is being remade into a willing servant of love. Love makes sexuality like a laser beam: its power under control, its intensity focused, nothing wasted or promiscuously scattered.

God began a comprehensive good work in you. He will complete what he has begun. Wrongs are made right, and, to quote Julian of Norwich, "all shall be well, and all shall be well, and all manner of thing shall be well."[1] You will flourish in a garden of safety and joy.

How can this ever be? We become so stained with lewd desire and our own transgressions. And the transgressions of others so darken us with hurt and fear. How can all wrongs be made right? Jesus, the merciful, steadily intervenes. To the indulgent, he brings forgiveness, covering perverse pleasures with new innocence. To the frightened, he brings refuge, the name that calms our fears and bids our sorrows cease. There is pleasure and protection in Christ, God's inexpressible gift. Sexuality becomes wise, and wisdom is that gift of God to which nothing else you desire can compare (Prov. 3:13–15).

The lovely quilt is an object lesson in creation and re-creation.

———

Needing a contrasting object lesson, I stopped in to talk with my auto mechanic. He fished a greasy rag from the trash bin at the back of his garage and handed it to me. Unnamable filth had soaked through that scrap of fabric. Ground-in, oily dirt. If your hands are clean, you don't really feel like touching such a sordid rag. If you must handle such an object, you pick it up by one corner between thumb and forefinger, holding it out away from you at arm's length. The filthy rag gives us a second, all-too-familiar picture of sexuality. Sex soaks up dark, dirty stains. We must face ground-in evils if we are to repair what's wrong with us and help others with what's wrong with them. You understand why Jude evokes an unpleasant sense of wariness even amid his call to generous-hearted love: "To others show mercy, mixed with fear—hating even the clothing stained by corrupted flesh" (Jude 23 NIV).

Greasy-rag experiences turn sex itself into a darkness of renegade desires, lingering hurts, haunting shame. The darkness and stain reside not in being created sexual beings but in the doubled evil of the human condition. Evils arise from within us; evils fall upon us. We misuse our bodies, and our bodies are misused by others.

How is your life turning out with regard to sexuality? A garden in the lattice? A greasy rag from the trash bin? Here is Jesus's personal purpose statement as he goes about his good work in us: "Behold, I am making all things new" (Rev. 21:5). This book explores that making new. But before we delve into the processes of that renewal, let me begin by identifying three orienting realities.

1

GETTING ORIENTED

In order to renew anything, we must have a vision for what it is intended to be, for what's gone wrong, and for how to bring about transformation. This chapter will establish that threefold vision for sexuality and then orient you to particular emphases in how I am coming at the issues.

A Threefold Vision

Christian Faith Revels in Sexual Fidelity

The Bible is frank about sexual joy within the circle of faithfulness. Fidelity first orients you as a child of God in relationship to your Father. You come under his care and oversight. Fidelity then orients you as a steward of your own body. We all enter adult life with the gift of singleness; many of us continue with the gift of singleness for many years, even a lifetime; and a majority of us will end life with the gift of singleness. We must be stewards of ourselves. Fidelity then orients you in relationship to your husband or wife, if God subsequently gives the gift of marriage. God made sex, defines sex, evaluates sex—just as he made communication, food, family, work, money, health, and every other good thing. In his design, the man and the woman went unclothed and celebrated a unity that was frankly physical. The blessing "Be fruitful and multiply" (Gen. 1:22, 28) would be realized by knowing one another "in the biblical sense," as sex used to be whimsically described. Passing this vision on, a wise father encourages his son:

> Let your fountain be blessed,
>> and rejoice in the wife of your youth,
>> a lovely deer, a graceful doe.
> Let her breasts fill you at all times with delight;
>> be intoxicated always in her love. (Prov. 5:18–19)

The Song of Solomon then sings with rhythms and images of sensual pleasure in the union of husband and wife. The Word of God chooses to spend whole chapters gazing in delight at male and female anatomy. Felicity and fidelity become one flesh.

When husband and wife join in intercourse, the One who sees in the dark sees exactly what they are doing and says, "It is very good." The private intimacy of marriage is public before the God who made male and female, who made their union good. Sexual intimacy is intended to flourish within trustworthy fidelity. It is meant to express love in the generosity and gladness of mutual giving. It bears fruit in children, if God gives that gift. The "one flesh" of marriage is such a good thing that it serves as a central metaphor for the relationship between Jesus Christ and his people. To see sexual immoralities as wrong is not to be nervous about sexuality. Christian faith envisions sexual joy before the eyes of the holy God. Neither immorality nor prudishness understands that.

CHRISTIAN FAITH IS CANDID ABOUT SEXUAL WRONGS

The Bible discusses many forms of sexual immorality and sexual victimization. A vision for fidelity does not drive honesty about infidelity and betrayal underground. Prudish? Not Scripture. Squeamish about the sordid details of human life? The biblical authors frequently (though not always) eschew photographic description and details when they speak of sex and sexual organs. They often model a certain delicacy of generic description. Nonetheless, they speak openly, sometimes even graphically, of rape, adultery, voyeurism, seduction, fornication, prostitution, homosexuality, gender bending, bestiality, incest, and the like.

When Tamar experienced betrayal, rape, and humiliation from her half-brother Amnon, we are not given videographic details. But we know what was done to her. When David played the voyeur from the palace walls, we are not given an itemized description of what his eyes took in. But we know what he was doing, and what he and Bathsheba subsequently did together.

To complain about the "sex and violence" in popular culture is to complain about the glorification, mislabeling, and voyeuristic detailing of such evils. It is not the fact that these dark human realities are on the table. The Word of God does not stint in describing sex, violence, and sexual violence. Genesis, Judges, 2 Samuel, and Proverbs capture sordid moments. But God labels sin and suffering accurately. He freely speaks of the sordid—as sordid. He does not titillate us with alluring lies and excessive pictorial detail. And God freely speaks of how alluring the sordid can be.

For example, Proverbs 7 tells a seduction story in vivid detail. But Scripture tells such a story to warn us of the allure. And whether the wrong is one-sided (e.g., rape) or two-sided (e.g., consensual immorality), sexual sin always proves suicidal. Genesis 19, Judges 19–20, and Proverbs 5–7 unpack that not just in principle but also through stories.

Scripture teaches constructive candor—the opposite of euphemism and evasiveness. It teaches accuracy—the opposite of titillation and brazen exhibitionism.

Christian Faith Brings Genuine Transformation

Jesus comes forgiving and changing the immoral. He bridges the chasm between sordid and glorious. He invites us to cross over from death to life. What was perverted can be converted. To disagree with immorality is not simply to condemn the immoral. It is to identify particular forms of lostness that need finding. We worship a seeking and finding God. We have been sought out and found by a Savior. He reproves the unruly in order to invite us to come seek help.

> Come now, let us reason together, says the LORD:
> though your sins are like scarlet,
>> they shall be as white as snow. (Isa. 1:18)

This same Jesus comes rescuing and protecting the victimized. He is a refuge for the afflicted. We worship a seeking and finding rescuer, a protector of the innocent. He calls predators, liars, and betrayers to account. He comes to deliver victims from the pain and power of what their oppressors have done.

> O LORD, you hear the desire of the afflicted;
>> you will strengthen their heart; you will incline
>>> your ear
> to do justice to the fatherless and the oppressed,
>> so that man who is of the earth may strike terror
>>> no more. (Ps. 10:17–18)

This Christ encourages the fainthearted and holds on to the weak.

> Be strong, and let your heart take courage,
>> all you who wait for the LORD! (Ps. 31:24)

In sum, the Lord has a highly positive view of sex. He has a highly negative view of immorality. And he has a deep concern both for the consensually immoral and for the victims of the criminally immoral. He has more mercy than we can imagine.

Of course, there are not two gospels, one for sinners and one for sufferers! There is the one gospel of Jesus Christ, who came to make saints of all kinds of sinner-sufferers and sufferer-sinners, whatever our particular configuration of defections and distresses. The proactive sins inflamed by immoral desires are significantly different from the reactive sins energized by fear and self-protection. But unbelief and lovelessness character-ize all of us, however vast the differences in how we express them. Similarly, the temptations that come by allure are signifi-cantly different from the temptations that come by affliction. But this world misleads and bedevils all of us, however vast the differences in what people face. So all of us head astray and all of us are led astray, but the paths we take and the provocations we face vary.

Jesus comes for each and all. So the dynamic by which the sexually immoral and the sexually victimized are transformed has a core similarity, though his work unfolds by many different ministry routes. Grace is not a panacea, a single message prescribed for whatever ails you. Christ comes bringing a myriad of specific remedies that address specific persons, struggles, and troubles. He always embodies steadfast love—and all that Exodus 34:6–7 promises. But like his Proverbs, he admonishes the sexually unruly, calling for a radical U-turn. Like the psalmists, he comforts the fainthearted, offering refuge and strength. Like a prophet, he brings justice, indicting oppressors and defending victims. Like a shepherd, he guides and protects, holding on to the weak. He is patient with all whom he befriends. In other words, he meets you right where you are. And he's always thinking about what you need to know and the next step you need to take.

Emphases of This Book

You've probably already noticed or sensed something a bit unusual about my approach in writing this book. Some books are written to help people who struggle with their immoral sexual impulses. Other books are written for people who struggle with the impact of sexual betrayal, molestation, and assault. But this book will intentionally look in both directions. Sin and affliction are different in kind. What you do and what happens to you could not be more distinct. But both intertwine in the DNA of the human condition. A double helix of darkness twists through all human experience.

Most books about sexual sanctification address the problem of sin, with little more than a nod to external forces that allure or afflict. And most books about sexual victimization are not about sanctification, giving little more than a nod to our instinctive unbelief and our impulse to react wrongly when we experience grave wrongs. But sanctification is about both transgressions and afflictions, and about the continual interplay between them. This is crucial, because it is true of both Scripture and life.

Another reason this is crucial arises from two key paradoxes in Christian growth. It is a decided mark of wisdom that our sins come to afflict us, not delight us. The experience of our own sin changes, so it becomes more like self-inflicted suffering. We experience what we want and how we behave as living contradictions to who we truly are. And it is a decided mark of wisdom that the sufferings that afflict us become occasions that produce growing faith, hope, and love. The experience of our suffering changes, so it becomes integral to how God frees us from our sins and teaches us wisdom. All Scripture—whether history or prophecy, psalm or proverb, Gospel or epistle—traffics in this interplay between our choices and our circumstances. Jesus untangles both sins and miseries. So I hope you find it helpful that I attempt to keep both in view.

You probably have not noticed something a bit more subtle about this book. The majority of books on the struggle with sexual immorality are written for men. The majority of books on the struggle with sexual victimization are written for women. And there is a partial truth in such emphases. There often is a disparity in the experiences of men and of women. And different pastoral priorities come into play when addressing two different kinds of struggles. But so far in this book, except for references to Scripture, my only use of male pronouns has been to designate my car mechanic; my only use of female pronouns has been to designate the artist who created our quilt. Of course, men and women are different. (That fact does have *something* to do with the topic of sex, after all!) But it is also true that sin and suffering, like faith and love, are not rigidly sex-typed. Men are not immune to molestation or rape; women are not immune to becoming sexual predators or using pornography. Men and women read the same Psalms and learn faith. Both sexes take Galatians to heart, receiving grace and expressing the fruit of the Spirit. The Great Commission tells us that the fundamental dynamics of human experience in relation to Christ's gospel operate across every nation, tribe, tongue, and people. But we can fail to notice that grace not only crosses cultures; it also crosses male-female differences. Mercies touch the wanderings and woes of every human heart.

Here's another significant thing about this book. It does not derive from theory. It arises from experience, my own and others'. Christ has touched the wanderings and woes of my heart. And my personal experience has been enriched and extended by thousands of candid conversations over more than forty years. I have listened carefully when people have spoken openly about their stories, their struggles, and their convictions. Most of these conversations have been with men and women seeking help. Many of these people have been shadowed by intrusive evils they've experienced. The reverberations of those betrayals have made life hard. And many people are greatly troubled by their erotic impulses. Their sexual desires and behavior distress them, rather than delighting and defining them. The truth is that they have a deeper core to their identity. The object of their sexual impulses is dissonant to who they are, contradicting core values and convictions. I have listened, understood what they are saying and why, and sought to help.

I have also been enriched by many significant conversations with people I love who are not seeking help. They are convinced that their sexuality is fine the way it is. They view their erotic desires and behavior as consistent with and even central to their core identity, values, and convictions. I listen, understand what they are saying and why, disagree, and still love them.

I've learned a great deal from firsthand life experience and from both kinds of conversations. I hope that the fruits of that experience bless you.

Finally, this book aims for explicit, unexpurgated righteousness. Fidelity and felicity make very good companions. I hope that these chapters deliver a clear vision and much grace, comforting the disturbed and disturbing the comfortable. The gospel of Jesus Christ renews us. He engages us in his work of renewing the immoral, the predatory, and the self-indulgent. And he engages us in the work of renewing the fearful, the withdrawn, and the overwhelmed. He is making faithful men and women.

A theme runs throughout the book: "I am sure of this, that he who began a good work in you will bring it to completion at the day of Jesus Christ" (Phil. 1:6). Notice that this sentence is not first about finding personal assurance. It communicates Paul's confidence regarding God's renewing work in other people, our brothers and sisters. Our Father has begun a process in you and in me that he will finish when we see Jesus Christ face-to-face. What will this lifelong process look like? How do we get from here to there? How does degradation transform into beauty? What's the battle like? We're somewhere in the middle, but the Spirit of life has begun a good work. And God always finishes what he begins.

2

MAKING RENEWAL

PERSONAL

Where do you struggle with sex? As with anger, self-righteousness, and anxiety, we are all deviants in some form or other. Some forms of sexual drift and distortion seem just a short step from normal. Wandering eyes? Romantic attraction and infatuation? A cautious chill in the presence of a flirtatious, aggressive, or mildly exhibitionistic person? And the more serious forms of deviancy and danger are never far away. You can hardly bear to put a name on what some people do or on what happens to some people. Has your sexuality become somehow unhinged, distorted, misdirected, darkened, or threatened?

The Wayward and the Wounded

Have you gone actively astray? Sexual sins are among the dark things that pour forth from within our hearts. When Jesus bluntly indicts a roster of wrongs (Mark 7:21–23), he calls out a wide range of sexual wrongdoings: sexual immoralities, adulteries, licentious behavior. And he names other general categories that can include sexual matters: evil thoughts, coveting, deceit, moral foolishness. This same Jesus offers costly mercy to the repentant. When you wash your dirty linen in the blood of the Lamb, you come out spotless.

Or has your sexuality been betrayed by someone else? Predatory people violate others in ways that cause lifelong pain. Jesus fiercely condemns the victimizers of innocence: seducers, users, deceivers, misusers, abusers, tempters (Matt. 18:6–7). The influential wrongs can be subtle as well as severe: provocative dress, suggestive speech or mannerisms. Being transgressed can bring fear, distaste, and shame about all matters sexual. Jesus offers the afflicted a merciful touch and safe refuge. God will wipe away every tear from your eyes. All fear, anxiety, and shame will one day be no more.

Or has your sexuality been doubly marred, both by your own transgressive desires and by the afflictions and temptations brought upon you by others? As with most human struggles, there is often an intricate dance between what arises from inside us and what assaults or beguiles us from the outside. Yes, a pornography user willingly chooses sexual immorality. But the everyday deluge of suggestive stimuli and the ready availability of erotic images make temptation a form of atmospheric pollution. And a girl or boy who was abused is an innocent victim of someone else's treacherous and malicious sexuality. But if that same child later becomes a promiscuous adult, he or she is culpable for that behavior. Life is complicated. We are enmeshed in unsettling realities. So Christ's grace sets out to do something more multifaceted than simply charging the unambiguously guilty and rescuing the unambiguously innocent. He enters sympathetically into the totality of human experience. He touches all our sins and all our afflictions.

Jesus's mercies make all things new. His grace is a most versatile stain remover. He redeems both the wayward and the wounded. His wisdom puts sex in its proper perspective. He goes to work on us. He works in us for as long as it takes. He does not give up. He will not give up on you.

Where are you in all this? The luminous quilt or the oily rag? A complex darkness or a garden of pure delights? Which picture best represents you, and why?

Stop and think about that for a moment.

It's not really a fair question! You probably can't answer either–or, because most likely you're somewhere in the middle, like me. We are people in process. That's important. This book is about identifying where you are. About knowing where you're heading. About asking for help. About helping you to take further steps in the right direction. This book is not about perfection. It is about *making* new, about *restoring* joys to the broken, about *washing* the dirtied. In other words, it's about an unfolding process of *becoming* wise and loving. It's about moving along a trajectory *away from* the darkness and *toward* the light.

So this book is about you on your journey into the garden of light.

There Is a Better Way

I recognize, of course, that many people aren't yet on the journey I have been describing. It is the easiest thing to become willingly mired in sexual darkness. What God calls "evil," decidedly transgressive people call "good," both to reassure their conscience and to convince others. What God portrays as slavery, they extol as freedom. People who defend doing what is wrong are not likely to have picked up this book or kept reading this far. They are not asking for help, not seeking forgiveness, not looking to be remade right. Their chosen lifestyle is a matter of personal preference and stated conviction.

But if you have been willingly mired in sexual sins and you have read this far, I suspect it is because some quiet voice is telling you, "There must be a better way. Something is off about how I am living." I hope you will read further. I hope you will find that what you want for yourself starts to change, that you come to see things in a different light, and that the seeming freedom to be yourself is actually a form of slavery and self-mutilation. I hope you will see that the things "everybody does" should not be done, and what seems like an identity to proudly affirm is a falsehood to recant. There is a better way.

Jesus Christ mercifully draws transgressors to himself. God thinks that our instinctive choices and opinions are wrongheaded.

> Woe to those who call evil good
> and good evil,
> who put darkness for light
> and light for darkness,
> who put bitter for sweet

and sweet for bitter!
Woe to those who are wise in their own eyes.
    (Isa. 5:20–21)

That's not just about sex. It's about everything that matters, in-cluding sex. Here's the background reality: "Each of us will give an account of himself to God" (Rom. 14:12). God is more than fair—he is also merciful. In fact, it's fair to say that Jesus Christ is *mercifully unfair*! "He does not treat us as our sins deserve" (Ps. 103:10 NIV). The Son of God came into the world to save sinners. You do not need to fear telling the truth about yourself. He already knows. He has come to bear our wandering and our woe that we might turn to him and find a new life that is filled with goodness.

Victims, too, are not automatically on the journey of renewal that I have been describing. Jesus mercifully draws those whom others have grievously wronged. The victims of betrayal and assault are often mired in a different sort of sexualized dark-ness. Trapped in a world of threat, shame, and despair, they don't know where to turn or how to go forward. They know of no garden of life protected within the lattice. They cannot imagine such a good place. They're unaware that there's a truer and better identity than "survivor"; that there's a truer safety than self-asserted boundaries; that trying to rebuild your life on self-trust, self-affirmation, self-protection, and self-assertion is not the way to truly recover from the distress of traumatic violation.

If this is you and you have read this far, I assume it is because you aren't satisfied with the diagnoses you've been given and the solutions you've been offered. They don't take you far enough. They aren't true enough. They don't bring enough light. I hope you will read further. When Jesus says, "Come to me, all who labor and are heavy laden, and I will give you rest," he means it (Matt. 11:28).

So Jesus invites both the sexually immoral and the sexually betrayed to turn in his direction. There is mystery at the heart of why any of us ever does seek him. Jesus said, "All that the Father gives me will come to me. . . . No one can come to me unless the Father who sent me draws him. . . . Everyone who has heard and learned from the Father comes to me" (John 6:37, 44, 45). There is a mystery behind why we start to see things in a different light. But you can be sure of this: if you seek him, he will be found by you. He is calling for you.

Walking toward Daylight

I assume that most of you who have read this far are already somewhere on the journey, already drawn to the light, however flickering and far away it might sometimes seem. Don't lose heart. No remnant darkness is so deep that it is immune to light.

Perhaps you've been grievously wronged sexually and have lived a nightmare. But you long for light. The longing for goodness and peace is a blossom of light pulling you in the direction of more light. *Kyrie eleison*—Lord, have mercy, you who bind up the brokenhearted. Jesus blesses those who hunger and thirst for everything wrong to be made right.

Or, perhaps you've been wrong sexually and have lived in a fantasyland of lewd, nude, and crude. But you feel sick and tircd, dirty and ashamed. Honest guilt and longing for good are blossoms of light. Your sins delight you less and less; they afflict you more and more. *Kyrie eleison*—Lord, have mercy, you whose mercies are new every morning. Whenever people know they need help from the Savior, then they're already walking toward daylight, not stumbling into darkness.

Are you tilted more toward light? Some readers will have walked far already. I hope this book does justice both to how you have already grown and how you still struggle. It is a great joy to remember what you once were, and to consider what you might have become, and to see where you are now, and to know that Jesus has begun his good work in you. Perhaps you have come far along this good path already. Perhaps you have been given much light sexually. Perhaps the garden of faithful self-control, of faithful pleasure, and of faithful gratitude for mercies is already budding or even flourishing in you. Perhaps the latticework of loving restraints and protections is set in place. O hopeful joy, so much has already been purified! *Gloria in excelsis Deo*; glory to God in the highest. But I know, and you know, that oily stains and cracked slats remain in the fabric of every person's life. We must still run the race of renewal.

A contemporary hymn contains this line: "In all I do, I honor you."[1] When I sing that hymn, I think, "Well, I *want* to honor you in all I do, Lord, but you know that I don't." The line is truest as a statement of honest intention and partial success, but untrue as a statement of perfected achievement. We want the garden, but grime still clings to us. Augustine memorably described his long struggle with wayward sexual desire:

As I prayed to you for the gift of chastity I had even pleaded, "Grant me chastity and self-control, but please not yet." I was afraid that you might hear me immediately and heal me forthwith of the morbid lust which I was more anxious to satisfy than to snuff out.[2]

It's not an easy fight, because some of the enemies of light reside in what animates our hearts.

Many less well-known saints have described their long struggle with being violated and have prayed along these lines: "Lord, free me from the grip of memories and the terror at what happened. How long must I remember? I am afraid that you do not hear me, and that you will not heal me forthwith of this pain and shame from which I so long to be set free." It's not an easy fight, because some of the enemies of light reside in what terrifies our hearts.

We want the latticework to protect us, but dark creatures slip into or out of our hearts. When talking about something as important and troublesome as sex, it is important to affirm that the desire for light is the beginning of the emergence of light.

On the last day, all will be light. Wayward impulses will have no say. Past failures will have no sting. Fears will be silenced. Dangerous people will be no more. But along the way, how does this divine redemption work out? How do you walk out this journey? We will consider many aspects of the journey and fight of faith in the chapters ahead. First, we must grasp the scope of the problems that need addressing.

3

RENEWING ALL THAT

DARKENS SEX

We fight on many fronts. There are many kinds of evil, more than we might first imagine. Some are obvious—some, not so obvious. So what are we up against? We face "enemies." The world, the flesh, and the Devil are the classic troika of intertwining foes of light mentioned in Ephesians 2:1–3.

In the context of Ephesians, "world" (*kosmos*) refers to the lies, false cultural messages, deceitful worldviews, seductive images, misleading role models, and peer pressures that swirl around us. Human beings who speak and live lies are powerful influencers. They are the everyday enemies of the light. Friends sleep around and live together without marrying. Pornography is three clicks away. Laws enforce the right to be immoral. Public opinion silences even principled discussion and disagreement.

"Flesh" (*sarx*) in Ephesians refers to the inner enemy, our own disordered impulses that generate lifestyle choices. A configuration of desires, fears, and false beliefs mislead us and animate us. We are too plausible to ourselves, willingly deceiving ourselves, suppressing the light of conscience, rationalizing what is wrong so that it seems like the most natural thing in the world. The lifestyle that unfolds can become habitual and assumed.

In Ephesians, the "Devil" (*diabolos*) emphasizes how a dark power works backstage in the world and in hearts. The Enemy gives lies and desires their uncanny, enslaving, blinding power. This deceiver and enslaver works hand in hand with social forces and the heart's impulses.

In sum, we are tempted and led astray by the plausible images and voices that surround us, by our own desires, and by the Tempter. The members of this troika can't be disentangled. All three work in concert, creating a fog of war, concealing their operations, enslaving willing participants. Sexual chaos is a complex affair.

And there's more. Other forces are also arrayed against the light. The distinctive emphases of Ephesians open the discussion but do not exhaust all that Scripture says about the forces that work on us.

"World" and "Devil" have another facet that does not appear in Ephesians. We face actual harm, as well as lies and false values. In the Psalms, *human* enemies are aggressors, predators, murderers, and liars. In 1 Peter, both human enemies and *the* Enemy are presented primarily as aggressors and oppressors. (Second Peter is about liars.) The world not only beguiles us with falsehoods; it also brings threats, betrayals, violations, pain, and dismay. And Satan is not only the liar who allures but also the murderer who stalks and afflicts. This violent reality is vivid for many people. As we have already described, many for whom sex becomes hard and dark are "more sinn'd against than sinning."[1] Tamar bore no blame for what Amnon did to her, but she lived in shame, grief, dismay, and isolation nonetheless (2 Samuel 13).

"Flesh" also has another face. The human heart is not only active in choosing evil but also self-reflective in bringing self-condemnation—and then active in silencing conscience. Conscience often contradicts a person's belief system and choices in unpredictable ways. Many people have waded deep into sexual license thinking there is no such thing as sin but have found themselves surprisingly smitten with guilt. It takes a lot of practice, propaganda, social reinforcement, persistence, and denial to sear the conscience.

Condemnation is the oddly contradictory dimension of human behavior that also affects how the world and the Devil operate. So, for example, Bill Clinton and Monica Lewinsky were two consenting adults doing sexual things in a culture that exalts personal choice in sexual matters. But they were publicly accused, besmirched, degraded, and (in his case) impeached. In parallel to public shaming and scolding, Satan works as the Accuser, alongside being a liar, Tempter, enslaver, and murderer. So the world, the flesh, and the Devil not only lead us astray; they also accuse and condemn us for straying. Experiences of self-condemnation, guilt, public humiliation, and shame are another part of darkened sexuality that calls for renewal.

Finally, there is one more very significant factor even beyond the multidimensional world, flesh, and Devil. Many hardships, heartaches, and pressures that people face do not involve any obvious malicious agent. Sickness, bereavement, financial hardship, political chaos, natural disasters, and death can afflict any one of us. We are not necessarily meant to take it personally and look for someone to blame. The "last enemy" and the shadows of death can significantly affect sexual feelings and behavior.

For example, a thirty-eight-year-old mother almost dies of a systemic infection after giving birth. By the time she recovers her health two years later, she has transitioned from being young, vivacious, and energetic to being old, worn, and slowed. Her sexual interest has vanished. Sex has become a mildly unpleasant chore, rather than a joyous marital delight. Her husband was thirty-four when she became sick, and has remained full of youthful passion for life. He starts looking around for a more lively partner and becomes a serial adulterer. He has no excuse at all. But a significant life pressure and loss has changed their marriage, providing a context in which he has sinned rather than learned the harder kinds of love and self-control.

So the world around us plays liar, aggressor, and accuser. The human heart generates both desire and condemnation. The Evil One lies, allures, murders, degrades, and accuses. And then there is all the ordinary affliction, disappointment, and loss. We have many knots to disentangle in the renewal of our sexuality. This chapter will focus on five specifics.

Unholy Desires

The most obvious forms of sexual darkness involve the sins of
overt immorality. There are countless ways that sexuality veers
into nonmarital eroticism. Sex can become a carnival of intoxi-
cating fires, a dreamworld of erotic arousal, predatory instinct,
manipulative intention, and the pursuit of carnal knowledge. In
a nutshell, in each of the many forms of wrong, a person copu-
lates with the wrong object of desire. Sexual love flourishes as
a loving intimacy between a husband and wife. But desires are
easily distorted and actions misdirected. Such miscopulation can
occur either in reality or in fantasy. These are the typical red-
letter, on-the-marquee sins.

So what do adultery, fornication, pornography, homosexuality, prostitution, rape, pedophilia, bestiality, voyeurism, incest,
fetishism, sadomasochism, transgenderism, and polyamory have
in common? You copulate, in person or in your imagination,
with the wrong object of desire.[2] Others become objects of unholy desire. Our culture earnestly tells us that the desires we discover within ourselves define us. Scripture is more realistic. By
impulse, orientation, inclination, tendency, habit, and instinct,
our desires mislead us. Sexual immoralities, either in fantasy
or in interpersonal transaction, are the obvious ways in which
human sexuality is misdirected into overt sins.

Scripture presents a broad-spectrum definition of sexual immorality. Because heterosexual marriage is the obvious norm
for sexual expression, adultery is the paradigm case for understanding sinful sexuality. Other deviancies are mentioned
occasionally—for example, incest, rape, voyeurism, bestiality,

homosexuality, transvestitism, prostitution, cohabitation, polygamy. They simply give us a representative sampling. Scripture never intends to be exhaustive (and never could be exhaustive, since sexual deviancy takes innumerable forms). For example, there is no mention of pornography in Scripture because print and electronic media did not exist to make it readily available. (Upper-class Romans did have a great deal of pornography in more durable, expensive forms.) But Jesus's comment that looking at a woman with lustful intent entails adultery of the heart easily generalizes. He did not need to mention the obvious extensions of his pithy words: a woman or a man looking at a man, a woman looking at a woman, an adult looking at a child, consensual sex between unmarried persons, pornography in any form, sexting, innumerable fetishes, and so forth.

I've heard arguments against the biblical sexual ethic that say, "There are only six Bible verses that mention homosexuality," and then proponents wiggle the definition of homosexuality to exclude modern forms. This is mere trivializing of Scripture. Narrowing Scripture's relevance to a verse count or the specific form of ancient practices neither establishes nor disestablishes right and wrong regarding sexual acts. God teaches us by identifying the main principle, giving us representative examples, and then expecting us to put in the effort to understand the "things like these" (Gal. 5:21) that are also obviously wrong.

The bold-print sins point in the direction of the fine-print versions of the same sins. Many varieties of flirtation, self-display, foreplay, and entertainment don't necessarily "go all the way" to orgasm. But suggestive remarks, crude humor, dressing to attract voyeuristic looks, erotic kissing, petting, and the like all intend in the direction of immoral copulation, whether they consummate their intention or not. Such behaviors (whether occurring in daily life or portrayed on screen or page) cross the line of love. Whether or not our cultural context views such things as acceptable, or even as entertaining, they are evils. Love considers the true welfare of others in "the eyes of him to whom we must give account" (Heb. 4:13).

Jesus Christ comes to those who have pursued unholy pleasures. He hates the gamut of perversities listed in previous paragraphs, and he is not ashamed to love and rescue sinners. He does not weary in the task of rewiring sexuality into a servant of love. He takes the initiative to bring forgiveness, and gives us countless reasons to turn. He freely forgives those who turn. He says, "You need mercy and help in your time of need. Come to me. Turn away from evil. Turn to mercies that are new every morning. Flee what is wrong. Seek help. Everyone who seeks, finds. Fight with yourself. Don't justify things that God calls wrong. Don't despair when you find evils within yourself. The only unforgivable sin is the self-righteousness that justifies sin and opposes the purifying mercies of God in Christ. Come to me. I will begin to teach you how to love."

Our culture asserts that any consenting object of desire is fair game for copulation. Individual will and personal choice are the supreme values. But Christ thinks differently, and he will get last say. That's important. "Let no one deceive you with empty words, for because of these things the wrath of God comes upon the sons of disobedience" (Eph. 5:6). Each of the distortions makes sex too important (and makes the Maker, evaluator, and Redeemer of sex irrelevant). Sex becomes your identity, your right, your fulfillment, your need. This is moral madness. Each ends up degrading sex as a merely natural urge that must find an outlet. That, too, is moral madness. Whether exalted or degraded, sex ends up disappointing, self-destructive, and mutually destructive.

Jesus brings sanity and good sense. Knowing God is always the primary good. Sex is like health, friendship, money, achievement, children, anger at wrong, and good weather. These are all good things that flourish only when they come second. God neither overvalues nor degrades the good things he has made. By realigning who you *most* love with all your heart, soul, mind, and might, he rightly orders all secondary loves.

When we think about the forms of "sexual brokenness" that need to be made new, it is natural to think first of the obvious sins. But other evils also begrime us as sexual beings. These also lie within the scope of redeeming love.

Unholy Pain

Many people experience pain and fear attached to sexual victimization. Have you been attacked or betrayed sexually? Even the thought of sex can become like the struggle of a burn survivor or a former soldier whose best buddy was blown up next to him. It can be a waking nightmare of hurt, fear, and helplessness. Jesus's kindness redeems both sinners and sufferers. He rights all wrongs. In previous pages we saw that Jesus is merciful to people who do wrong. He is also merciful to people who are done wrong. In both cases, he brings the kinds of mercy that change a person. When you are used, misused, and abused, sex becomes very dark.

The erotic is meant to be expressed as one kind of mutual loving-kindness. Sex thrives in a context of marital commitment, safety, trust, affection, giving, closeness, intimacy, and generosity. It flourishes as a normal form of love within marriage. A husband and wife are "naked and . . . not ashamed" with each other and under God (Gen. 2:25). They give mutual pleasure. Sex with your spouse can be simple self-giving, freely given and freely received. Sexual interactions can express honesty, laughter, play, prayer, and ecstasy. Marital sexuality is open before the eyes of God, approved in your own conscience, and approved by family and friends who care for you before God.

But sex can become extremely distasteful and frightening. Harassment, groping, seduction, bullying, predation, attack, betrayal, and abandonment are among the many ways that sex becomes stained by sufferings at the hands of others. When you've been treated like an object, the mere thought of the act can become filled with tense torment. Immoral fantasies bring one poison into sex. Nightmarish memories infiltrate with a different poison. The experience of violation can leave the victim self-labeled as "damaged goods." Sex becomes intrinsically dirty, shameful, dangerous. Even in marriage, it can become an unpleasant duty, a necessary evil, not the delightful convergence of duty and desire.

If such things happened to you, you might well feel hatred, terror, and disgust. You might feel guilt, shame, and self-reproach over what someone else did to you. Your thoughts of sexual relations might be filled with loathing and despair, the furthest thing from lustful desire, and the furthest thing from simple love. Painful fear, like pleasurable lust, is a greasy rag. To those for whom sexual experience has resulted in unholy pain, Christ basically says: "I understand your experience. Psalm 10 captures how a victim of predators cries out for help. I hear the cries of the needy, afflicted, and broken. I am your refuge. I am safe. I will remake what is broken. I will give you reason to trust, and then to love. I will remake your joy." With reason, two-thirds of the psalms engage the experience of those who suffer violence, violation, and threat. These sufferings found their point of reference in the God who hears you now; who is your refuge, your hope; who is willing to hear your anguish and loneliness; who overflows with comforts. The reference point makes all the difference. God cares and will patiently repair what has been torn.

In different ways, both violator and violated are stained with the wrong of a fallen world. In different ways, Jesus Christ washes both. And there is still other darkness, and there are other fresh mercies.

An Unredeemed Sense of Guilt

The human conscience is a like a fine musical instrument. When in tune, it plays lovely music. When out of tune, it sounds wrong notes. A conscience rightly oriented has three characteristics:

- What is the standard? You evaluate yourself (and others) by God's standards of right and wrong.

- Who is the judge whose opinion matters? How God views you matters more than how you view yourself (self-esteem) or how others view you (reputation).
- Where do you turn when you fail? You rely on God's mercies in Christ.

Experiences of sexual darkness bring disorientation to the conscience. We will look at two problems: the self-righteousness of a seared conscience and the self-condemnation of an anguished conscience.

First, a dull or seared conscience is a deadly affliction. Many sexual behaviors are misbehaviors, but the conscience feels no guilt or shame. Instead, wrongdoing is defended and even extolled as normal and desirable—the wrong standard. Appeal is made to the authority of personal desires and popular opinion—the wrong judges. There is no need for mercy because people are okay as they are—self-salvation by self-righteousness is assumed. The conscience reassures itself, "Peace, peace," but there is no peace. The operations of the conscience fail the test of reality on all three counts. But God can take such a heart of stone and make such a person come to life.

Second, an anguished conscience is an exceedingly painful affliction. Feelings of guilt and shame become stuck in a vortex of self-condemnation. Rightly aroused guilt and shame are good gifts of God. They signal that something is wrong. Guilt senses failure against a standard that matters; shame senses failure before the eyes that matter. These feelings are natural, God-given repercussions when our conscience is alive to genuine personal failure before God. But guilt and shame are meant to go somewhere good.

What do you do when you find yourself drowning in self-condemnation? The normal aftermath of doing wrong (or thinking you have done wrong) is to feel guilt, shame, regret, and remorse. But what comes next? We are meant to seek and find mercy and refuge in the loving welcome of our Father. But when we are not alive to the mercies of Christ, what follows is a predictable cycle of repetitive self-reproach, resolutions to change, self-punishing penance, attempts to forgive ourselves, hollow rationalizations, trying to make up for the wrong by compensating actions, self-concealment, escapism to numb pain and shame, and, finally, despair.

Consider two self-condemnation scenarios. What happens when the conscience is accurate—for example, "My girlfriend and I were wrong to do that"—but blind to the mercies of God? Right standard, right judge. But this true sense of guilt spirals in many fruitless directions. And what happens when the conscience is inaccurate? For example, "I should have done something to avoid being sexually abused. It must have been my fault. I feel horrible about myself and ashamed to let anyone know." Wrong standard, wrong judge. And self-blame for wrong reasons is inevitably blind to God's mercies, so it spirals in further fruitless directions. The second scenario calls for a more comprehensive reorientation of the conscience, but both forms of self-condemnation need to find the mercies of God.

Consider a situation where actual sin has occurred. An unmarried man and woman have not treated one another respectfully, as brother and sister, but have indulged in heavy petting. They know they've done wrong. But, like many strugglers, they oscillate between moments of obsession with erotic pleasure and days of obsession with moral failure. Guilt turns them inward.

But grace invites them out of themselves. So simple to say, so hard to do. We routinely underestimate how radically faith relies on fresh mercies freely given. Grace means that what makes things right comes to this brother and sister from outside themselves. It's a sheer gift from their Father and their Savior given courtesy of the Holy Spirit. They don't get it by self-laceration, by trying to work up a different set of feelings, by trying to say it's not that big a deal, by resolutions to do better, by distracting themselves. They are forgiven, accepted, and saved from death *by God's mercy*. Listen to how Scripture shows a person dealing candidly with his former and current sins. The italics highlight how much his hope amid guilt lies outside himself:

> *Remember*, O LORD, *Your* compassion and *Your*
>   lovingkindnesses,
> for they have been from of old.
> *Do not remember* the sins of my youth or my
>   transgressions;
> According to *Your* lovingkindness *remember* me,
> For *Your* goodness' sake, O LORD.
> . . . .
> For *Your* name's sake, O LORD,
> *Pardon* my iniquity, for it is great. (Ps. 25:6–7, 11 NASB)

David's sexual sin was high-handed. It tore his conscience (Psalms 32, 38, 51). It brought immediate and long-lasting consequences (2 Sam. 12:10–12, 14–15). Yet David was truly forgiven (2 Sam. 12:13). He experienced the joy of repentance and the wisdom, clarity, and purposeful energy that real repentance brings—captured in those same psalms and the rest of 2 Samuel 12. Notice how David radically appeals to the quality of "*Your* compassion . . . lovingkindnesses . . . goodness . . . O LORD." David's own conscience remembers only too well what he did. But he appeals to what God will choose to remember. In effect, "When God looks at me, will he remember my sin or his own mercies? O LORD, when you think about me, remember yourself." Understanding these last few sentences will forever change your experience of failure.

So let's make it personal. Are you haunted by your sins in the eyes of God, in the eyes of your conscience, and in the eyes of others who might find out? Your sin may have just occurred a few minutes ago; or it may be a distant but potent memory. Perhaps you don't commit that sin anymore. You've come far and no longer feel any allure to a lifestyle you once avidly pursued. Or perhaps you just did it again. But the memory—whether fresh-minted or ancient history—fills you with dismay. Perhaps immediate and long-term consequences of your sin run far beyond the repercussions within your conscience: abortion, STD, inability to bear children, ongoing vulnerability to certain kinds of temptations, a bad reputation, ruined relationships, wasted time, failed responsibilities. Nobody did this to you; you did it to yourself. The sense of shame and dirty distaste haunts your sexuality just as it haunts those who were victimized. Only you victimized yourself (and others you betrayed). You, too, feel like damaged goods. Sex is not bright, iridescent, cheerful, re-strained, generous, matter-of-fact. It is not a flat-out good to be enjoyed with your spouse, or saved should you ever marry.

You might live with such guilty feelings in your singleness. You might have brought them into your marriage. Perhaps you are afraid of relationships, because you know from bitter ex-perience that you can't be trusted. Perhaps it's hard to shake off the train of bleak associations that attach to sexual feelings and acts.

Just as sin and suffering turn us in on ourselves, so guilt and shame spiral inward. But living repentance and faith turn outward to the one whose opinion most matters. What God chooses to "remember" about you will prove decisive. Your conscience, if well tuned, is secondary. (This retuning is the core dynamic in renewing an inaccurate conscience.) Your self-evaluation depends on the evaluation he makes and the stance he takes. If the Lord is merciful, then mercy gets final say. It is beyond our comprehension that God acts mercifully *for his sake*, because of what *he* is like. Wrap your heart around this, and the typical aftermath of sin will never be the same. You will stand in joy and gratitude, not grovel in shame. You'll be able to get back about the business of life with fresh resolve, not just with good intentions and some flimsy New Year's resolutions to do better next time. This is our hope. This is our deepest need. This is our Lord's essential and foundational gift.

You need to know how faith in Christ's mercy decenters you off of yourself and re-centers you onto the living God's promise and character. You know other people who need to know this.

We typically mishandle the aftermath of sin with further forms of the God-lessness that manufactures sin. The One "to whom we must give an account" freely offers mercy and grace to help us by the loving-kindness of the Lord Jesus Christ (Heb. 4:13–16).

We've considered sin, suffering, guilt, and shame. These obviously call for renewal, and the need is easily accessible theologically. The next two needs for renewal that I will discuss are of a different order. They are areas of concern that are easy to overlook.

Not Just a Male Problem

It should be obvious that sexual sins allure and entangle both men and women! After all, adultery is the archetypal defection. In adultery's inversion of Genesis 2:25, the man and the woman are both naked and are shameful. But when the church discusses "struggles with sexual lust," the implicit or explicit assumption is often that this is basically a problem for Christian men. Seductive women ("out there") may be viewed as sources of temptation. But erotic lust is seen as a typically male problem. But what about Christian women? There are some typical differences between men and women, but there are also core similarities when it comes to lust.

For starters, the Bible is candid that there is no temptation that is not "common" to all (1 Cor. 10:13). This doesn't mean that temptations always take exactly the same form, but there are underlying commonalities. We struggle with the same kinds of things, though we may struggle in somewhat different ways. We should not assume that females are categorically incapable of the same unvarnished, immoral eroticism that characterizes some males. It takes two in any act of adultery or fornication. The female may well be the initiator/aggressor in sending out sexual signals or in arranging a liaison. Women have roving eyes and get hooked on erotic pleasures. Women masturbate. Women adopt a homosexual lifestyle. A woman can pattern her identity around fulfilling sexual self-interest and having a magnetic effect on male sexual interest. When she finds mercy in Christ and starts her journey toward the garden of light, her struggle may directly parallel the struggle of a man who has similarly patterned his lifestyle around immoralities. Both must learn how to love, rather than how to fulfill and arouse lust.

Second, it's noticeable that female sexuality in America has taken on cruder forms in recent decades (or, at least, is far more brazen). Open lewdness and unabashed immorality have replaced coy, suggestive hints of availability. Male or female, if you want it, go for it. For example, female athletes increasingly adopt the openly obscene behaviors that were once the prerogative of male athletes: gutter humor, mooning, streaking, sexualized hazing and initiation rites, predatory sexual acts, and general grossness. Using obscene language, attending a strip show, and surfing pornographic websites are not exclusively male sins. Women's magazines routinely serve up advice on how to have wildly ecstatic sex with your "partner" of choice. Marital status and gender are optional categories, irrelevant to whether or not to be sexually active. Living together outside marriage—fornication—is so normal that it raises neither eyebrows nor qualms of conscience.

But Jesus Christ is "no respecter of persons." An immoral female is in the same condition as an immoral male. The degradation of sex is gender-blind, and Jesus's self-sacrificing mercy works with both females and males to transform sex into an expression of love, light, and fruitfulness (Eph. 5:1–10).

Third, there are some typical and noteworthy differences between men and women. Both strugglers and those who minister to them should be aware of variations on the common themes. At the level of motive, for example, male sexual sin and female sexual sin often operate in somewhat different ways. An old joke plays off the difference between simple and complex eroticisms:

Question: What is the difference between men and women?
Answer: A woman wants one man to meet her every need,
   while a man wants every woman to meet his one need.

Men are often more wired to visual cues and to anonymous "body parts" eroticism. Women are often more wired to feelings of personal intimacy and emotional closeness as cues for sexual arousal. But notice the "often" in those sentences. These aren't absolute differences. They describe bell curves that can slide one way or the other. But being aware of potential differences is important. The motives driving adultery, fornication, and promiscuity may follow quite different patterns.

Homosexuality provides a particularly obvious example of these differences. Lesbians frequently are on a different trajectory from male homosexuals. Many lesbians I know were once actively, unambivalently heterosexual, whether promiscuous or faithfully married. They might have conceived, borne, and raised children without much questioning of their sexual idenlity. But over time the men in their lives proved disappointing, incommunicative, uncomprehending, drunken, unfaithful, or violent—or all of the above. Perhaps during the unhappiness of a slow marital disintegration, or while picking up the wreckage after a divorce, other women proved to be far more understanding and sympathetic friends. Emotional intimacy and communication opened a new door. Sexual repatterning as a lesbian came later, often the result of a slow process of experimentation that followed emotional closeness.

In this common scenario, the life-reshaping "lusts of the flesh" were not initially sexual. Instead, cravings to be treated tenderly and sympathetically—to be known, understood, loved, and accepted—played first violin, and sex per se played viola. A frequent core dynamic in lesbianism is a desire for intimacy running out of control and over the cliff into eroticism.

In male homosexuality, the core dynamic is more often sexual desire running out of control. Again, notice my use of "frequently," "often," and "common." This comparison is not absolute. I've known male homosexuals for whom desires for social acceptance (or for domineering power) played first violin, and erotic desires were a secondary correlate. And I've known lesbians who were predatory, seductive, and domineering in pursuing erotic partners. What the Bible terms "lusts of the flesh" include many different kinds of desires that run amok, hijacking the human heart.

Given some of these variations, it's no surprise that lesbians tend to form more stable relationships and tend to be less promiscuous than male homosexuals. It's also no surprise that homosexual ideology rarely attempts to make the argument that female homosexuality is genetic, though it has often attempted that argument about men. Raw, obsessive sexuality seems to invite biological rationalizations in a way that a more multi-factored relationship doesn't. I've heard a number of homosexuals, both male and female, make comments along the following lines: "It's just easier to be gay. You don't have to bother with the whole male-female game. If men mainly want sex, let them find each other. If women want to be known, understood, and loved, let them build relationships with each other. You can avoid the hassle of trying to bridge the male-female divide in relationships. It's easier to get what you want with the same sex. And you can have simpler friendships with the opposite sex, too, when you take the sex thing off the table."

Fourth, the culture of romance and the obsessions of women's magazines do not draw nearly as much attention as male-oriented pornography. Men do graphic pornography. That's an obvious problem. Women do romance. It's the same kind of problem, though the participants keep their clothes on a while longer, and there's more of a story to tell before they tumble into bed. Romance is female pornography. The sin comes wired through intimacy desires first and builds toward erotic desire. The formulaic fantasies offer narrative emotion candy, not visual eye candy. Romance tells a story about someone with a name, someone you fall in love with. It builds slowly. It's more than a moment of instant gratification with anonymous, naked, willing bodies. The romantic novel genre has even made a crossover to evangelical Christian publishing houses. The sex is cleaned up;

the knight in shining armor is also a deep spiritual leader who marries you before sleeping with you. But the fantasy appeal to intimacy and romantic desires remains as the inner engine that allures readers.

And women increasingly do outright pornography, both literary and visual. Like male pornography, there is a progression from soft-core to more openly erotic to frankly pornographic writings that target women. The readers and viewers of *50 Shades of Grey* are reported to be 75–80 percent female.

Female versions of sexual-romantic sin are as much shop-floor rags as are male versions. Jesus Christ calls all of us out of fantasy, delusion, and lust, whether the fantasyland is filled with naked bodies or with romantic knights. Jesus Christ is about the reality business. An old prayer gets things straight: "Grant that I may not so much seek . . . to be loved as to love."[3] Jesus teaches us how to be committed, patient, kind, protective, able to make peace, keeping no record of wrongs, merciful, forgiving, generous, and all the other hard, wonderful characteristics of grace. He teaches us to consider the true interests of others. He teaches us a positive, loving purity that protects the purity of others. Instead of our instinctual ways—narcissism, fascination with our own desires and opinions, self-indulgence—Jesus Christ takes us by the hand to lead us in ways that make *vive la différence* shine brightly.

Sexual Struggles within Marriage

We mislead ourselves and others if we say or imply that getting married solves the problems of sexual sin, temptation, pain, guilt, shame, and confusion. All sorts of sins can carry on within marriage. All sorts of remnant heartaches and fears can still play out. "Making all things new" continues to renew sex within marriage. Here are some examples.

One person may need to learn that sex is good, not dirty. You can relax rather than tense up. You can give yourself freely, rather than worry about what will happen to you. Pleasure will not betray you. Your spouse is faithful and can be trusted. Only larger, deeper, fundamental trust in God can free us to grant simple trust and generous love to another human being who will in fact let us down sometimes and will do us wrong in some ways.

Another person may need to learn whole new patterns of sexual arousal. Willing nymphomania, copulatory gymnastics, and oral sex may have turned on your fantasies and fornications. But your spouse, God's gift to you, may enjoy quiet, tender moments being held in your arms. The Richter scale of raw ecstasies may have spiked higher in your past immoralities than in your marriage. But you need to learn that the scale of solid joys and lasting treasures proves incomparably deeper and more satisfying.

Another person may need to learn that sexual bliss is not the *summum bonum* of human life and the essence of love. Throughout a marriage, you or your spouse may struggle, in sex as in other areas, and both of you will need to learn that "love is patient" comes first in Paul's description for a reason (1 Cor. 13:4). You always need to say no to immoral lust. You will also need to restrain normal sexual desire during some seasons for a variety of reasons: advanced pregnancy and postpartum difficulties; forced separation because of business or military; a chosen fast from sex because of more pressing needs; the diminution of sexual desire and arousal with advancing age; consequences of prostate cancer, vaginal prolapse, or other conditions; the loss of your spouse. Sexual intimacy may even come to an end years before death parts a husband and wife. Will they still love each other?

Another person may struggle with painful memories attached to sex because of rape, child abuse, and other aggressions. Renewal and building trust can be a very slow process.

Still other marriages may need to give up destructive relational patterns: game playing, manipulation, giving to get, avoidance, bartering sex for other goodies, sulking. Even high-stakes criminal sins—sadistic sexual aggression, violence, and rape—can occur in marriage.

Still other people must alter the mental link that equates sex with success or failure, with performance, and with identity. As Christ redefines and re-centers your identity, he changes what sex *means*. Sex can become a simple and meaningful way to give. It can become a simple pleasure, as normal as eating breakfast. It can become a safe place where failures and struggles can be talked about and prayed through.

Some marriages may deal with a lack of sexual responsiveness: impotence and frigidity in the older terminology; "erectile dysfunction" and "arousal disorder" in the clinical jargon. On the male side, Viagra, Cialis, and Levitra offer a purely chemical solution for symptoms. The problem can have a significant biological component unrelated to normal aging. But biology is always entangled with spiritual issues: performance anxiety, an unwillingness to face the diminishments of aging, finding identity in being sexual, the separation of sex from love, guilt over premarital sex, or unreal expectations of potency that have been learned from the media, pornography, or previous fornication.

Still others may face temptations to make comparisons with previous partners, or with fantasy partners, or with some idealized fantasy of what marital bliss should be like. Wise sex loves *your* husband or wife.

Still others will continue to struggle with familiar patterns of lust. They may be tempted to flirt, or to cheat, or to view pornography, or to masturbate in the shower, or to fantasize about past experiences.

Finally, every person will struggle with garden-variety anger, anxiety, grumbling, selfishness, and unbelief. And every person feels the weight of life's difficulties. The everyday nonsexual sins and troubles don't disappear! Other sins and hardships can clutter the bedroom with nonsexual troubles that greatly affect sexual intimacy. Christ's ongoing mercies will remake your sexuality in part by remaking worry and irritability (and the rest) that arise in response to life's pressures.

You get the picture! Marriage is not a garden of uncomplicated sexual delights. God who began a good work in you will bring his purposes to completion on the day of Christ Jesus. His redemption will touch *every* form of darkness. We can't do justice to "sexual brokenness" or bring mercy unless we get the whole problem on the table. Jesus works with us. And it is our joy that he works with far more than just the Technicolor sexual immoralities.

That is a lot of darkness to consider! And it raises such poignant need for hope and renewal. There are no quick fixes. But there is something much better. In the next chapter we will look at the time frame in which the renewing process unfolds.

4

RENEWAL IS LIFELONG

One key to fighting well is to lengthen your view of the battle. If you think that one week of "shock and awe" combat will win this war of redemption, you're bound to be disappointed. If you're looking for some magic, an easy answer, a one-and-done solution, then you'll never really understand the nature of the honest fight. And if you promise easy, once-for-all victories to others, then you'll never be much help to other strugglers.

God works organically in our lives. Organic growth has integrity. God works step-by-step. He walks with you. He's always interested in how you take your very next step. Walking through life with him feels right. You're going somewhere. The day of "completion" will not arrive until the day when Jesus Christ arrives (Phil. 1:6). When we see him, then we will be like him (1 John 3:2). Only when God lives visibly in our midst will all tears be past (Rev. 21:3–4). Someday, not today, everything being renewed will be entirely new (Rev. 21:5). Much of the failure to fight well, befriend well, pastor well, and counsel well arises because we don't really understand and work well with this long truth.

Consider two specific implications. First, sanctification is a direction you are heading. Second, repentance is a lifestyle you are living.

Sanctification Is a Direction

Often our practical view of sanctification, discipleship, and counseling posits a monochromatic answer and takes the short view. If you memorize and call to mind one special Bible verse, will it clean up all the mess? Will the right kind of prayer life drive all the darkness away? Will remembering that you are a child of God and justified by faith shield your heart against every evil? Will developing a new set of habits take away the struggle? Is it enough to sit under good preaching and have daily devotions? Is honest accountability to others the decisive key to walking in purity? Will careful self-discipline and a plan to live constructively eliminate the possibility of failure?

These are all very good things. But none of them guarantees that three weeks from now, or three years, or thirty years, you will not still be learning how to love rather than lust. We must have a vision for a long process (lifelong), with a glorious end (the last day), that is actually going somewhere (today). Put those three together in the right way, and you have a practical theology that's good to go and good for the going.

Look at church history. Look at denominations. Look at local churches. Look at people groups. Look at families. Look at other people. Look at the people in the Bible. Each has a history and keeps making history because the challenges that sanctification faces do not end. As Martin Luther sang, "In much the best life faileth," and so all of us must "live alone by mercy."[1] And as John Newton sang:

> Through many dangers, toils, and snares
> I have already come,

because

> grace has brought me safe thus far,
> and grace will lead me home.[2]

Look at yourself. In this life, we can never say: "I've made it. No more forks in the road. No more places where I might stumble and fall flat. No more hard, daily choices to make. No more need for daily grace." Life never operates on cruise control. The living God seems content to work in his church and in people groups on a scale of generations and centuries. The living God seems content to work in individuals (you, me, the person you are trying to help) on a scale of years and decades, throughout a whole lifetime. At every step, there's some crucial watershed issue. What will you choose? Whom will you love and serve? There's always something that the Vinedresser is pruning, some difficult lesson that the Father is teaching the children he loves (John 15; Hebrews 12). It's no accident that "God is love" and "love is patient" fit together seamlessly. God takes his time with us.

In your sanctification journey and in your ministry to others, you must operate on a scale that can envision a lifetime, even while communicating the urgency of today's significant choice. *Disciple* is the most common New Testament identity describing God's people. A disciple is simply a lifelong learner of wisdom, living in relationship to a wise master. The second most common identity, *son/daughter/child*, embodies the same purpose. By living in lifelong relationship to a loving Father, we learn how to trust and love in practical ways day by day.

When you think in terms of the moral absolutes, it's *either* oily rag *or* garden of delights. But when you think in terms of the change process, it's *from* oily rag *to* garden of delights. We are, each and all, on a trajectory from what we are to what we will be. The moral absolutes rightly orient us on the road map. But the process heads out on the actual long, long journey in the right direction. The key to getting a long view of sanctification is to understand *direction*. What matters most is not the distance you've covered. It's not the speed you're going. It's not how long you've been a Christian. It's the direction you're heading.

Do you remember any high school math? "A man drives the 300 miles from Boston to Philadelphia. He goes 60 mph for 2 hours and 40 mph for 3 hours, then sits in traffic for 1 hour not moving. If traffic lightens up and he can drive the rest of the way at 30 mph, how many hours will the whole trip take?" If you know the formula "distance equals rate times time," you can figure it out (8 hours!). Is sanctification like that, a calculation of how far and how fast for how long? Not really. The key question in sanctification is whether you're even heading in the direction of Philadelphia. If you're heading west toward Seattle, you can drive 75 mph for as long as you want, but you'll never, ever get to Philadelphia. And if you're simply sitting outside Boston and have no idea which direction you're supposed to go, you'll never get anywhere. But if you're heading in the right direction, you can go 10 mph or 60 mph. You can get stuck in traffic and sit awhile. You can get out and walk. You can crawl on your hands and knees. You can even get temporarily turned around and head the wrong way for a while. But you get straightened out again. At some point you'll get where you need to go.

The rate of sanctification is completely variable. We cannot predict how it will go. Some people, during a season of life, *leap like gazelles*. Let's say you've been living in flagrant sexual sins. You turn from sin to Christ, and the open sins disappear. No more fornication: you stop sleeping with your girlfriend or boyfriend. No more exhibitionism: you stop wearing that particularly revealing blouse. No more pornography: you stop surfing the net or reading the latest salacious romances. No more adultery or homosexual encounters: you break it off once and for all. Never again. It sometimes happens like that. Not always, of course, but a gazelle season is a joy to all.

For other people (or the same people at another season of life) sanctification is a *steady, measured walk*. You learn truth. You face your fears and step out toward God and people. You learn to serve others constructively. You build new disciplines. You learn basic life wisdom. You learn who God is, who you are, how life works. You learn to worship, to pray, to give time, money, and caring. And you grow steadily—wonder of wonders!

Other people (or the same people in another season) are *trudging*. It's hard going. You limp. You don't seem to get very far very fast. Old patterns of desire or fear are stubborn. But if you trudge in the right direction—high praises to the Lord of glory! One day, you will see him face-to-face. You will be like him.

Some people *crawl* on their hands and knees for a long or short season. Progress is painful. You're barely moving. But praise God for the glory of his grace, you are inching in the right direction.

And there may be times when you're not even moving—stuck in gridlock, broken down—but you're still *facing* in the right direction. That's Psalm 88, the "basement" of the Psalms. The writer feels dark despair—but it's despair oriented in the Lord's direction. In other words, it's still faith, even when faith feels so discouraged you can only say, "You are my only hope. Help. Where are You?" That kind of prayer counts—it made it into the Bible.

There are times you might fall *asleep* in the blizzard and lie down, comatose and forgetful—but grace wakes you up, reminds you, and gets you moving again. There are times you slowly *wander* off in the wrong direction, beguiled by some false promise, or disappointed by a true promise that you falsely understood. But he who began a good work in you awakens you from your sleepwalk, sooner or later, and puts you back on the path. And then there are times you revolt and do a *face-plant* in the muck, a swan dive into the abyss—but grace picks you up and washes you off again, and turns you back. Slowly you get the point. Perhaps then you leap and bound, or walk steadily, or trudge, or crawl, or face with greater hope in the right direction.

We love gazelles. Graceful leaps make for great stories about God's wonder-working power. And we like steady and predictable. It seems to vindicate our efforts at making the Christian life work in a businesslike manner. But, in fact, there's no formula, no secret, no technique, no program, no schedule, and no truth that guarantees the speed, distance, or time frame. On the day you die, you'll still be somewhere in the middle. But you will be further along. When we lengthen the battle, we realize that our business is the direction. God manages to work his wonder-working power in and through *all* of the above scenarios! God's people need to know that so someone else's story doesn't set the timetable for how Christ's grace is working out in your life.

By the way, everything I've just discussed applies in every area of life, not just with the renewal of sexuality.

Repentance Is a Lifestyle

What was the first trumpet call of the Reformation?

It was not the authority of Scripture, foundational as that is. Scripture does reveal the face and voice of God. As Jesus says, "Whoever has seen me has seen the Father" (John 14:9). A Person shows through the pages. You learn how he thinks. How he acts. Who he is. What he's up to. You are gripped by the intimate and universal relevance of Scripture to all things human. But Scripture alone did not stand first in line.

It was not justification by faith, crucial as that is. We *are* oily-rag people. Christ *is* the garden of light. We *are* saved by his doing, his dying, his goodness. We are saved from ourselves outside of ourselves. No religious hocus-pocus. No climbing up a ladder of good works, or religious knowledge, or mystical experience. He came down, full of grace and truth, Word made flesh, Lamb of God. We receive. That's crucial. But faith alone wasn't actually where it all started.

It was not the priesthood of all believers, revolutionary as that is. Imagine, there aren't two classes of people: the religious people, who do holy things by a special call from God, and the masses of laity toiling in the slums of secular reality. The "man of God" is not doing God's show before an audience of bystanders. We all assemble as God's people, doing the work and worship together, with differing gifts. The one Lord, our common King and attentive audience, powerfully enables faith and love. Yes and amen, but this radical revision of church didn't come first.

The trumpet call, thesis number 1 of Luther's Ninety-Five Theses, was this: "When our Lord and Master, Jesus Christ, said 'Repent,' He called for the entire life of believers to be one of repentance." That dismantled all the machinery of religiosity and called us back to human reality. Luther glimpsed and aimed to recover the essential inner dynamic of the Christian life. It is an ongoing change process. It involves a continual turning motion, turning toward God and turning away from the riot of other voices, other desires, other loves.

We tend to use the word *repentance* in its more narrow meaning, for decisive moments of realization, conviction of sin, confession, seeking mercy. But Luther also intends us to understand the word in its wider, more inclusive meaning. Transformation, growth, maturing, and renewal of mind and lifestyle involve a continual process of *metanoia*, an ever-changing, ever-developing wisdom. We turn *from* what comes naturally and turn *to* the faith, love, and joy that are found in knowing Jesus Christ. John Calvin put it in a similar way: "This restoration does not take place in one moment or one day or one year. . . . In order that believers may reach this goal [the shining image of God], God assigns to them a race of repentance, which they are to run throughout their lives."[3] The entire Christian life (including the more specific moments of repentance) follows a pattern of turning from other things and turning to the Lord.

This wider notion of *metanoia* brings many surprising fruits. For example, for a victim to learn to find refuge in God takes a patient renewal of mind and heart. Turning from terror, shame, fruitless remembering, and self-protection is a gradual process. There is a gradual process of learning to know and trust that if people do unspeakable evil against me—even if they assault, enslave, and torture me—the Lord is good and does good. Such a fundamental alteration never happens in a single moment of insight. It comes through a growing intuition and embrace of the reality that can say, for instance: "Psalm 23 speaks truly of my experience. When I walked through the valley of the shadow of death, I felt all alone. But I have come to know that the Lord is with me."

Luther went on to write a beautiful statement describing the transformation dynamic that occurs as we live *from–to*:

This life is not righteous, but growth in righteousness; it is not health, but healing; not being, but becoming; not rest, but exercise; we are not yet what we shall be, but we are growing toward it; the process is not yet finished, but it is going on; this is not the end, but it is the road; all does not yet gleam in glory, but all is being purified.[4]

Lifelong progressive sanctification was the trumpet call back to biblical faith. It was a call back to *this* life—including sex—in which the living God is on scene throughout your life. He planned a good work. He began a good work. He continues a good work. He will finish a good work. He has staked his glory on the completion of that work. Lengthening the battle heightens the significance of our Savior for every step along the way. We are not yet what we shall be, but we are growing toward it.

5

RENEWAL IS A

WIDER BATTLE

Sexual sin and sexual victimization grab everyone's attention. Immorality is red-letter sin; abuse is red-letter suffering. They haunt the conscience and excite the gossip. They can push other sins and afflictions into the background. They go up on the marquee in red letters ten feet high.[1]

But consider our struggle with sin and suffering this way. Imagine a multiplex theater screening many movies simultaneously. Immorality or violation might be the "feature film" advertised on the marquee. But other significant films are playing in other screening rooms. The war with sin, the experience of affliction, and the triumph of grace take place in many places simultaneously.

In ministry to someone who struggles with sexual darkness, you may get the breakthrough in another screening room, in an area that neither of you had noticed or considered to be related. A fresh understanding of God's intimate purposes in suffering can significantly rewrite the script of a person's life. A breakthrough—dealing with anger, or pride, or anxiety, or laziness—may have ripple effects that eventually help disarm the big bogeyman that has been hogging all the attention and earnest concern.

It's very important to widen the battlefront and not to let the high-profile wrongs blinker us from seeing the whole picture. The following case study shows how sexual sin can and must be located within wider battles.

"My Temper Tantrum at God"

Tom is a single man, thirty-five years old. You might be able to fill in the rest of his story, because his pattern is so typical! He came to Christ, with a sincere profession of faith, when he was fifteen. At about the same time, his twenty-year struggle with sexual lust began. It involves episodic use of pornography and episodic masturbation, about which Tom is deeply discouraged. Over the years he has experienced many ups of "victory," and just as many downs of "defeat."

Tom sought help from me as his elder and small group leader. He was discouraged by recent failures, by the latest downturn in a seemingly endless cycle. Over the years he had tried "all the right things," the standard answers and techniques. He'd tried accountability—sincerely. It helped some, but not decisively. Accountability had a way of starting strong but slipping to the side. At a certain point, to tell others you failed yet again, and to receive either sympathy or exhortation, stopped being helpful. Tom had memorized Scripture and wrestled to apply truth in moments of battle. It often helped, but then in snow-blind moments, when he most needed help, he'd forget everything he knew. Sex would fill his mind, and Scripture would vanish from sight. Other times he would just override the truth in an act of "Who cares?" rebellion. Then he'd feel terrible; his conscience would only go snow-blind for half an hour at a time!

He'd prayed, and he continued to pray. He fasted. He sought to discipline himself. He planned constructive things to do with his time, and to do with and for others. He'd gotten involved in ministry to teens. He tried things that aren't in the Bible: vigorous exercise, cold showers, dietary regimes. Briefly, he even tried the advice of a self-help book, trying to think of masturbation as "normal, something everybody does, so give yourself permission." His conscience, wisely, could never get around Jesus's words in Matthew 5:28 about committing adultery in your heart.

Tom had tried it all. Most things (except giving up the fight) helped a bit. But in the end, success was always spotty and fragile. Tom had gained no greater insight into his heart and into the inner workings of sin and grace. For twenty years it had been "Sin is bad. Don't do it. Just do [x, y, or z] to help you not sin." His entire Christian life had been conceived and constructed around this struggle with episodic sexual sin.

His pattern was as follows. Seasons of relative purity might last for days, weeks, even a few months. He measured his success by "how long since I last fell?" The longer he'd go, the more his hopes would rise: "Maybe now I've finally broken the back of my besetting sin." Then he'd fall again. He'd stumble through seasons of defeat, wandering back to the same old pigsty. "Am I even a Christian? Why bother? What's the point? Nothing ever works." He was plagued with guilt, discouragement, despair, shame. Sometimes Tom would even turn to pornography to dull the misery of his guilt over using pornography. He'd beg God's forgiveness over and over and over, without any relief or any joy. Then, for unaccountable reasons, the season would change for the better. He'd get inspired to fight again. In one such season, he gave me a call. He really wanted deliverance once and for all.

How could I help Tom? I was reticent to simply give him more of the same things he'd tried dozens of times and found wanting. I didn't want to just give him a pep talk and a Scripture, urge him to gird his loins to run the race, and offer accountability phone calls. What was he missing? What was happening in the other theaters of his life? Were there motives and patterns neither of us yet saw? What was going on in the days or hours before he stumbled? What about how he (mis)handled the days and weeks after a fall? Why did his whole approach to life seem like so much complicated machinery for managing moral failure? Why did his approach to the Christian life seem so dehumanized and depersonalized? His Christianity seemed like a big production, a lot of earnest effort at self-improvement. Why did his collection of truths and techniques never seem to warm up and invigorate the quality of his relationships with God and people? Is the centerpiece of the Christian life really an endless cycle of "I sin. I don't sin. I sin. I don't sin. I sin." What were we missing?

I asked Tom to do a simple thing, attempting to gain a better sense of the overall terrain of his life: "Would you keep a log of when you are tempted?" I wanted to know what was going on when he struggled. When? Where? What had just happened? What did he do? What was he feeling? What was he thinking? If he resisted, how did he do it? If he fell, how did he react afterward? Did anything else correlate to sexual temptations?

Through all the ups and downs, Tom maintained a disarming sense of humor. He laughed at me, and said, "I don't need to keep a log. I already know the answer. I only fall on Friday or Saturday nights—usually Friday, since Saturday is right before Sunday."

If you have any pastoral care genes in you, you light up at an answer like that. Repeated patterns always prove extremely revealing on inspection. I asked, "Why does sexual sin surface on Friday night? What's going on with that?" He said, "I turn to pornography as my temper tantrum at God."

Amazing! Look what we just found out: another movie was playing in a theater next door. Suddenly we were not only dealing with a couple of bad behaviors: viewing pornography and masturbating. We were dealing with *anger at God* that was driving those behaviors. What was that about?

Tom went on to give a fuller picture: "I come home from work on Friday night, back to the apartment. I'm all alone. I imagine that all my single friends are out on dates, and my married friends are spending time with their wives. But I'm all alone in my apartment. I build up a good head of steam of self-pity. Then by nine or ten o'clock, I think, 'You deserve a break today'—I even hear the little McDonald's jingle in my head, and then sexual desires start to look really, really sweet. 'God has cheated you. If only I had a girlfriend or a wife. I can't stand how I feel. Why not feel good for a while? What does it matter anyway?' Then I take the plunge into sin."

Amazing, isn't it? Pornography and masturbation had captured all the attention, generated all the guilt, defined the moment and act of "falling." Let's call that screening room 1. But then we also heard about anger at God that preceded and legitimated sexual sin: screening room 2. We heard about hours of low-grade self-pity, grumbling, and envious fantasies about his friends and fellow workers: a matinee performance in screening room 3. We heard Tom name the original desire that led to self-pity, to anger at God, and finally to sexual lust: "God owes me a wife. I need, want, demand a woman to love me." That was playing in screening room 4, an unobtrusive G-rated film, seemingly no problem at all. It was a classic nonsexual lust of the flesh that Tom had never viewed as problematic. In fact, in his mind, it was practically a promise from God: "Psalm 37:4: 'Delight yourself in the Lord, and he'll give you the desires of your heart.' If I do my part, God should do his part and give me a wife."

As Tom and I kept talking, I found out why God owed him a wife: "I've tried to do all the right things. I've served him. I've tried accountability. I've memorized Scripture. I've tried to be a good Christian. I do ministry. I witness. I tithe. . . . but God hasn't come through." In other words, the "right answers" for fighting sin are also the levers to pry goodies out of God.

Tom's words sound eerily like the self-righteous whine of the older brother in Jesus's parable of the prodigal son: "I'm good, therefore God owes me the goodies I want." Subsequent anger at God operates like any other sinful anger: "You aren't giving me what I want, expect, need, and demand." This fatally flawed, proud "upside" of the classic legalistic construct was showing in screening room 5. And why did Tom mope in self-lacerating depression for days and weeks after falling, rather than finding God's living mercies new every morning? That's the self-punitive, despairing "downside" of the legalistic construct: "I'm bad, therefore God won't give me the goodies." Screening room 6 was where self-punishment, self-atonement, penance, and self-hatred played out.

It doesn't take much theological insight to see how all these distortions of Tom's relationship with God express different forms of basic unbelief. They suppress living knowledge of the true God. They create a universe for oneself void of the real God's presence, truth, and purposes. Unbelief does not mean a vacuum; rather the universe fills up with seductive, persuasive fictions. Screening room 7 was showing a blockbuster that Tom had never noticed as trouble. (When Dame Folly keeps her clothes on and quietly erases awareness of God, she is invisible.)

In fact, we even found out why Tom was so eager right then to get my counsel and advice. Why did he want to have victory over his lust problem, to try again, to defeat the dragon of lust once and for all? He had his eye on an eligible young lady who started to attend our church. And that reawakened his motivation to fight. If only lust would go, then God would owe, and maybe Tom would get the wife of his dreams. Even his agenda for seeking pastoral counsel played a bit part in the wider battle: screening room 8!

Wider Battle, Greater Progress

Look how far we'd come in half an hour. Tom's "fall" at 9:30 p.m. last Friday was not where he'd started to fall. It was not even his most devastating fall. For me to assist Tom's discipleship to Jesus was not simply to offer tips and truths that might help him remain "morally pure" on subsequent Fridays. Counseling needed to be about rewiring Tom's entire life. "Cure of souls" is what ministry does.

You can see why we must widen the battlefront in order to cure souls. Tom concentrated all his attention on one marquee sin that surfaced sporadically, defining and energizing all his guilty feelings. But that narrowing of attention served to mask far more serious, pervasive sins. As a pastor, friend, or other counselor, you don't want to concentrate all your energies in the same place Tom did. There were other, deeper opportunities for grace and truth to rewrite the script of this man's life. Tom had turned his whole relationship with God into flimsy scaffolding. Self-righteousness ("victory at last") would get him the goodies he really wanted out of life. Though Tom knew and professed sound theology, in daily practice he reduced God to "an errand boy to satisfy [his] wandering desires" (as Bob Dylan voiced it).[2]

Tom and I put the fire of truth and grace to the scaffolding and rebuilt his faith. Wonderful changes started to run through his life. We didn't ignore temptations to sexual sin, but many other things that he had never before noticed became urgently important. We spent far more time talking about self-pity and grumbling as "early warning" sins, about how the desire for a wife becomes a mastering lust, about how the self-righteousness construct falls before the dynamics of grace. Temptations to sexual sin diminished significantly. They were not erased, but the topography of the battlefield radically changed. The significance of Jesus Christ's love went off the charts. The lights of more accurate and comprehensive self-knowledge came on. A man going in circles, muddling in the middle, started to do some leaping and bounding in the right direction. We experienced the delights of a season of gazelle growth.

Ministering to someone who has struggled for twenty years with the exact same thing is disheartening, and frequently a recipe for futility. Ministering to someone who is starting to battle a half-dozen foes that were previously invisible is extremely heartening! Widening the war served to deepen and heighten the significance of the Savior who met Tom on every battlefront.

6

RENEWAL IS A

DEEPER BATTLE

The Bible is always about behavior, but it is never only about behavior. God's gaze into human nature always gets below the surface, into the "thoughts and intentions of the heart" (Heb. 4:12), what we believe and what we pursue. His gaze and Word expose the implicit reality map, the covert purposes and goals, the desires and fears, the things we intuitively believe about God, self, others, health, suffering, the purpose of life, and a hundred other critical realities. We may be aware, semi-aware, or wholly unaware of the inner masters that shape the way we approach life, view people, and respond to circumstances.

In this chapter we will primarily examine some underlying dynamics of sexual immorality. Throughout this book I have sought to consider the redemption of sex holistically, keeping both sin and suffering on the table. But the book is short, and the topic vast. So here we will look mainly at sin. But at the end of the chapter, we will also consider some of the deeper dynamics that emerge when the context is suffering.

An immoral act or fantasy—behavior—is a sin in itself. But such behavior always arises from desires and beliefs that dethrone God. Whenever I do wrong, I am loving *something besides God* with all my heart, soul, mind, and might. I am listening attentively to *some other voice*. Typically (but not always!), immoral actions arise in connection with erotic desires that squirm out from under God's lordship. But immorality results from many other motives, too, and usually arises from a combination of motives.

We saw some of this in describing Tom. Erotic motives, the "feel good" of sex, played an important role. But other motives—"I want a wife"; "if I'm good, God owes me goodies"; "I'm angry because God has let me down"—interconnected with his eroticism. Many coconspirators played a role when Tom started rummaging in the gutter of "I want to look at naked women" and "I need sexual release now." Many other lusts join hands to give a boost to sexual lust.

It's worth digging into the patterns of motivation both to understand yourself and to minister wisely to other people. As our understanding of sin's inner cravings deepens, our ability to know and appreciate the God of grace grows deeper still. Consider a handful of typical examples to prime the pump.

Motives at Work in Sexual Transgressors

Angry desires for revenge. Sexual acting out can be a way to express anger. I once counseled a couple who had committed backlash adulteries. First they had a big fight, full of yelling, threats, and bitter accusations. In anger, the man went out and slept with a prostitute. Still burning with anger, he came home and gloated about it to his wife. In retaliatory anger, the woman went out and seduced her husband's best friend. Did they get any erotic pleasure out of those acts? Probably. But was *eros* the driving force? No way.

Though it's rarely that dramatic, anger frequently plays a role in immorality. A teenager finds sex a convenient way to rebel against and to hurt morally upright parents. A man cruises the Internet after he and his wife exchange words. A woman masturbates to fantasies of former boyfriends after she and her husband argue. In all these situations, the redemption of dirtied sexuality can only happen alongside the redemption of dirtied anger.

Longings to feel loved, approved, affirmed, valued through romantic attention. Consider the situation of an overweight, lonely teenage girl with acne, whose enjoyment of sex as an act is minimal or even nil. Why then is she promiscuous, giving away sexual favors to any boy who pays her any attention? She barters her body not in service to erotic lust but in order to feed her consuming lust to have someone care and pay her romantic attention. When boys say sweet things and pledge their faithful love, she might even know inside that they are lying. She knows that they are merely using her as a receptacle for their lust, but she temporarily blocks out the thought. She does sex anyway—because she's hooked on "feeling loved." Ministry to such a young woman does her a disservice if we only concentrate on the wrong of fornication and do not help her to understand the subtler enslavement of living to get attention.

She is an extreme case. But many people, especially early in their becoming "sexually active," are significantly pressured by desires to be acceptable, by fears of rejection, by desires to be loved in nonsexual ways. Sexual behavior can be an instrument in the hands of nonsexual cravings. After all, the wrong in our desires is often not what we want—being cared for and finding sexual pleasure are both good things. The evil twist comes when we want it too much. All that goes wrong needs the mercies and transforming power of Christ.

Thrilling desires for the power and excitement of the chase. Some people enjoy the sense of power and control over another person's sexual response. The flirt, the tease, the Don Juan, the seducer are not motivated solely by sexual desires. Often evil erotic pleasure is enhanced and complemented by deeper evil pleasures: the chase, the hunt, the thrill of conquest, the rush that comes with being able to manipulate the romantic-erotic arousal of another. There is a kind of sadistic pleasure driving through such sexual sins. Perpetrators like to see people get aroused, "fall" for them, and squirm. They may become indifferent to a willing sexual partner once that particular chase has ended. Repentance and change for seducers will address lusts for perverse power and excitement, as well as lusts for sex.

Anxious desires for money to meet basic survival needs. The obvious link of sex to money is the "sex industry." Sex makes lots of money for lots of people. As in the previous cases, *eros* may be one factor. But in money-making sex, pleasure plays second fiddle to mammon.

There are also more subtle situations. A single mother in our church was in very tight financial straits. She found herself strongly tempted by her sleazy landlord's offer of free rent in exchange for sexual favors. If she had fallen, sexual desire might have been nonexistent. In fact, she might have fornicated despite feeling active repugnance, shame, and guilt in the act. To God's glory, she opened up her struggle to a wise woman. In a variety of appropriate ways, the church was able to come to her aid with care and counsel. One aspect of care for her came from the deacons (who didn't even know what almost happened): "Know that you will not end up on the street. We are your family. If you get stuck, if you wonder where the money will come from for rent, or groceries, or a doctor's bill, don't think twice about asking for help."

Interesting, isn't it? Mercy ministry to financial needs played a significant role in reducing a woman's vulnerability to one particular sort of sexual temptation. She needed counsel, too, in order to run further in her race of repentance. But anxiety, finances, and the character of God were more salient than her sexual temptation.

Distorted messianic desire to help another person. Certainly there are pastors and priests who are sexual predators, but that's not the only dynamic when sexual sin infects ministry. I've dealt with a number of situations that involved the very impulses that make for ministry—impulses, though, that ran far off the rails.

For example, I got to know a middle-aged couple with a ministry of taking in troubled young adults. The wife ended up sleeping with one of the young men because she felt so sorry for the degree of loneliness, rejection, and abandonment he had experienced. She was mortified when she came to her senses, and came as her own accuser. We were able to restore the marriage, but it was a cautionary tale.

Here's another example. A pastor feels deep concern for a lonely young widow or divorcée. He so much (too much) wants to help her and comfort her. She so appreciates his wise, scriptural counsel. He's such a role model of kindness, gentleness, communication, attentive concern. But life is still very hard and lonely for her. He starts to console her with hugs. They end up in bed. The motives? Sexual, yes. But more significant in the early going was a warped desire to be helpful, to be admired, to make a real difference, to be important, to "save" her.

When anyone who is not the Messiah starts to act messianic, it gets very ugly very fast. If you minister to a minister who has committed sexual sin, you might find that sex was only the poisoned dessert. The poisonous entrée might be a very different set of deceitful desires, desires arising more in the mind than from the body (Eph. 2:3; 4:22).

Desires for relief and rest amid the pressures of life. Sexual sin often serves as an escape valve from other problems. When steam pressure gets too high in a pressure cooker, it blows off steam. That's a metaphor for what's often true with people, too.

Consider a man who faces, and mishandles, extreme pressures in his workplace. He's part of a team facing a drop-dead deadline for a major project. They've been running behind. He's had a month of eighty-hour work weeks. He's harried, driven, preoccupied, worried, worn out. Every day his boss applies more pressure, more panic, more threats. There's been vicious infighting on the project team: who's responsible for what task, who's to blame for what glitch, who gets credit for what achievement. All along, he is not casting real cares on the God who cares for him (see 1 Pet. 5:7); he is not "anxious for nothing" (Phil. 4:6 NASB) but anxious about lots of things.

After two straight all-nighters, the team finishes the project— just under the wire. They've made it. He's made it. Success. Finally he has a free night, with no deadlines, no jungle of intramural combat, no tomorrow to worry about. But after a month of living "stressed-out," he feels no relief. He finds no satisfaction in achievement. So he surfs the Internet, revels in pornography, and forgets his troubles. What's going on with him?

Erotic sin is part of his picture, but there's a lot more. Every deviant motive—whether lust of the flesh, lie, or false love—is a hijacker. It mimics some aspect of God. It usurps some promise of God. Consider that about two-thirds of the psalms present God as "our refuge" in the midst of the troubles of life. Amid threat, hurt, disappointment, and attack, God protects, cares, and looks out for us. Our friend has faced troubles: people out to get him, threats to his job, intolerable demands, relentless weeks. But he's been finding no true refuge during this frenzied month. Now, in a spasm of immorality, he takes false refuge in eroticism. His erotic behavior serves as a counterfeit rest from his troubles.

Psalm 23:4 breathes true refuge:

Even though I walk through the valley of the shadow
   of death,
  I will fear no evil,
for you are with me.

But the man in our example flees to false refuge, saying in effect: "After I've walked through that godforsaken valley of the shadow of death, I will fear no evil, because the photograph of a surgically enhanced female wearing no clothes is with me." A false refuge looks pretty silly when it's exposed for what it really is.

Indifference, cynicism, "Who cares?," "What's the use?" Wanda was a single female seminary student beginning her second year of studies. She came in to talk with me in early September. She'd been a Christian for five years, having come to faith at age thirty. The previous fifteen years had been highly sexualized: a series of live-in boyfriends, and promiscuous hooking up in between more-steady boyfriends. During the past summer Wanda had fallen twice into sexual immorality. Both were one-night stands with a coworker at the restaurant where she was waitressing. She knew with every fiber of her being that what she'd done was wrong. She saw exactly how in the moment of temptation she had willfully silenced her conscience and turned away from God. She was deeply grieved at her failure of self-control.

Why did Wanda do it? There were the predictable situational factors that make a person vulnerable. She was working late. She was tired after a long shift. Her roommate was away for the weekend, so there was no one to notice how late she came in. She felt lonely. When she looked in the mirror, she was noticing the creases of worry, fatigue, and aging on her brow, and the crow's feet around her eyes. She had turned thirty-five. The waiter was twenty-something, good-looking, carefree, funny, flirtatious, and sexually uninhibited. She knew he was danger. She knew he was temptation. And in the moment when he said, "Let's go do something after work," she said to herself, "Oh, what does it matter? I don't care." She went out for a drink and ended up in his bed. The "Who cares, what's the use?" attitude is a powerful behavior-altering drug.

When pastors in the ancient church noted and discussed the seven deadly sins, they recognized the attractive power of sexual immorality—*concupiscentia*. They also recognized the hypnotic power of indifference, of giving up, of not caring, of sloth, of becoming weary, of the shrug that says, "Whatever"—*acedia*. It is worth recovering an awareness of *acedia* as a dynamic that can operate on the inside of many behavioral sins: gluttony, binge watching TV, video-game obsession, dope smoking, drinking, and licentiousness.

Sexual sin is symptomatic. It expresses that deeper war for the heart's loyalty. We've looked at a handful of different ways the deeper war operates. There are other dynamics, too! But I hope this primes the pump so you learn to recognize more of what's going on inside when red-letter sins make an appearance.

Motives That May Tempt the Victimized

This deeper war for the heart's attention, trust, and primary love also rages in everyone who has ever been wronged, assaulted, seduced, or abused. The human heart is a factory of desires, fears, and false beliefs. Here's a sampler of some typical motives that may be operating in people who have been betrayed and victimized. Snapshots of contrasting motives appear in parentheses:

- I crave safety, protection, and refuge, and I create my own through avoidance, keeping hard boundaries, and never being vulnerable to anyone. ("The Lord is my refuge" —see Pss. 11:1; 18:2; 73:28; 91:9)

- I want revenge. Angry thoughts and bitter talk about men in general fill my mind and conversations. ("Beloved, never avenge yourselves, but leave it to the wrath of God"—Rom. 12:19)

- I desperately look for someone who will love me, and I continually test anyone who tries. ("Fear not, for I am with you"—Isa. 41:10)

- I buy beautiful clothes, fill my house with beautiful possessions, invest thousands in beauty products, and carefully craft the image and face I present to the world. ("Consider the lilies"—Matt. 6:28)

- I repeat self-affirming mantras to boost my self-esteem and self-confidence. ("If God is for us, who can be against us?"—Rom. 8:31)

- I ingest pills and alcohol to make the pain go away. ("The Father of mercies comforts me in all my affliction, so that I am able to comfort others who are in any affliction"—see 2 Cor. 1:3–4)

- I have given up in despair and cynicism. ("Set your hope fully on the grace that will be brought to you at the revelation of Jesus Christ"—1 Pet. 1:13)

If you have suffered sexual violation, you were a victim during that act. But in the aftermath, where do you set your hopes for healing? Where do you turn? What voices do the talking in your head? How do you understand who you are? There is a universe of difference between "I am a victim of abuse" and "I am a child of God who experienced evil at the hands of someone who betrayed my trust." There is an eternity of difference between "I am a survivor" and "I am beloved of Jesus and am finding refuge and hope in the Lord of life."

Learning to see more clearly is a crucial part of our sanctification journey. Teaching others to have eyes open to the deeper battles is a crucial part of wise pastoral ministry. Jesus Christ looks better and better the more we see what he is about. He is not simply in the business of cleaning up the embarrassing moral blots. Understanding the deeper battle for our hearts deepens the significance of the Savior. He alone sees your heart accurately. He alone loves you well enough to make you love him.

7

RENEWAL BRINGS AN INCREASINGLY SUBTLE STRUGGLE

A newcomer to war imagines that the first battles are the hardest battles. When you're first coming out of the morass of an adulterous relationship, of being betrayed by a spouse's adultery, of promiscuous fornications, of having experienced rape or molestation, of a homosexual lifestyle, or of an obsession with Internet porn, it can seem like your troubles will be over if you can only get past what you did or what someone else did to you. You or someone else insulted God. It sucked the life out of you. You are left either with a devouring "insect lust" for sexual sin (to quote Dmitri Karamazov)[1] or with a smothering fear of being betrayed.

Those first battles are hard. But if you take a significant step forward, will your troubles be over? That's not how life works. That's not how sanctification works in the cleanup from sexual darkness. In fact, in some ways it's the opposite. The more obviously destructive sins and sufferings can actually be "easier" to deal with. The subtler sins can be more stubborn, pervasive, sneaky, and elusive.

Consider a metaphor for this. Many computer and video games send you out on a quest, a sort of pilgrim's progress. You proceed through level after level, facing test after test, until, say, at level 40 you've run the race and won. Level 1 starts you out with easier challenges. The tasks are clear cut. The enemies are slower, more limited in their abilities, more obvious in their approach, not so smart. With some practice, you learn to accomplish your task and blow away your attackers. Level 2 gets a little harder. Each successive level gets harder still. The tasks get trickier. The enemies are wilier, stronger, quicker, more numerous. The skills you need are subtler and more varied. If you ever arrive at, say, level 32, it's because you've died often, but you've learned something each time, and you've kept coming back. You've come a distance in the right direction.

In this chapter, I will concentrate first on sanctification amid the subtleties of sexual sin, and then touch more briefly on sanctification amid the subtleties of our response to suffering. I will lead with the increasingly subtle struggle against immorality, and then point out the parallels in the struggle with being victimized. The struggle with sexual sin (as with any other sin) has a certain similarity to those video games. There is typically a front-and-center issue, and the "front lines" of the current battle move from the more overt sins to subtler sins.[2] Let's work out the metaphor.

Levels of Subtlety of Sexual Sin

HIGH-EFFORT, HIGH-COST SINS

Think of consenting sex (adultery, fornication, homosexuality, bisexuality, prostitution) and criminal sex (rape, child abuse) as the level 1 sins. These are the obvious evils. I don't mean that such sins are easy to break or easy to change. But they are relatively easy to see. Easier to recognize as wrong. Easier to know when you're doing wrong, once your conscience starts to see straight. And such sins are usually harder to do and harder to get away with.

Think about that. You have to involve other people. You have to hide things from people who love you, who would be unhappy to find out what you're doing. You have to tell consistent and increasingly complex lies in order to get away with it. You have to lie to your own conscience to persuade yourself that everything's okay. Because these actions involve actual copulation with other people, those partners may blow your cover, or blackmail you, or slip up, or report you. These sins can catch up with you very quickly, taking you down in an instant. They can destroy your reputation. Destroy family relationships. Destroy finances. Destroy health by a sexually transmitted disease. Even send you to jail. In other words, these sins take a lot of work and can bite back hard. If you're willing to seek mercy and change, it's easier to set up meaningful barriers against the high-effort, high-cost sins.

Jesus Christ often begins his work of mercy and renewal by

dealing with such high-handed sins. Often the dramatic first steps of sanctification shake off overt evils. Oily-rag people make leaps and bounds into the garden of light. There are adulterers who repent and never again have sexual relations with anyone other than their own spouses. It is entirely possible to have lived an immoral life for many years, with a string of lovers, and then to make a complete break with that sin in the level 1 sense. That does not always happen. And it's never a snap of the fingers. And you may still face ongoing consequences. And believers do fall back into such sins. But grace and change can be as visible and as powerful as the sin once was. Accountability relationships can really help. The Scriptures openly and frequently speak into the obvious sins to bring transformation. (By doing this, God also familiarizes us with how the subtler versions of sin and love work, teaching us how to see more of life for what it is and can become.)

LOWER-EFFORT, LOWER-COST SINS

Let's say you've done some growing. You've put away overt evils. No immoral liaisons. By grace you've worked and fought your way to a level 8 battle. Pornography was around before, but now it's the biggie. In some ways, pornography is a tougher problem than adultery. In one sense, it's "not as bad," because it doesn't involve an accomplice or obvious victim. But it's harder to get rid of. And setting up protective barriers is harder.

Why is this? Pornography is easier to do and easier to get away with. The necessary deceit is not as complicated. It doesn't take much work for you to do the sin. Adultery usually takes a lot of effort, both to arrange and to cover your tracks. But pornography? The gap between temptation and sin can be a matter of seconds. Three clicks of the mouse, and you're there. Standard fare in films. A remote control in your hand to check out what's on cable TV. And who's to know? No one. Pornography use is harder to discover. Unless you fail to erase it off your computer. Or you spend so many hours online late at night that friends and family get suspicious. Or someone walks in on you. Or you get depressed and grouchy because you feel guilty. Or your relationships slowly fray and alienate because of your preoccupation, defensiveness, and hiding. The consequences are shameful, but usually not as disastrous as with the immediately interpersonal sins.

So pornography is both "not as bad" as adultery and yet harder to defeat because it's easier to do and not quite as devastating. Christ is merciful here, too. Many people have significantly broken with pornography—usually with a fight, usually with losing some skirmishes, usually with some recidivism. In the long run, they've never gone back, or the stumbles are increasingly rare. You learn the joys of righteousness and the deeper pleasures of a clear conscience and honest relationships. You learn to say no to yourself. You become more interested in good things. You care about people, and sin just doesn't have as much room to insinuate itself into your heart. Some practical tools can help, too. A friend who will look you in the eye, ask a direct question, and expect an honest answer can help you. You can set up Covenant Eyes software to monitor your Internet use and email a report to a friend.

No-Effort Sins

Let's say you've put immoral copulation and pornography in the rearview mirror. The acted-out sins no longer own you. Are there no more enemies to fight? Now we're up to level 16: memories and mental videos. This is an even subtler problem. You don't even have to *do* anything. No effort, no expense. You aren't copulating outside of marriage. You aren't cruising the Internet. But you have a theater and library in your own mind. It's all stored there: memories, images, stories. Within your mind's reach are things you did, experiences you had, people you knew or watched or read about. You don't have to tell any lies or arrange anything. You just open a door in your mind. You can't get caught—except by the Searcher of hearts, before whose eyes all things are open and laid bare, him "to whom we must give account" (Heb. 4:13). Because he sees us on the inside, and because he's merciful both inside and out, grace is available here, too.

Sometimes the battle with the archive of mental videos stalls because you actively cherish and nurture old memories. But when you actually start to fight, you wish you could push "erase" and obliterate the collection of old videos. But the erase button on memories doesn't work on request. You face a subtler battle: learning to say no inside your mind and yes to your Father, who is right at hand. The point is clear. The enemies get subtler. They aren't as bad outwardly. But they're worse when it comes to getting rid of them, because mental sins are so easy to arrange and not so immediately self-destructive.

Sins That Come Looking for You

Let's say you've left adultery and pornography behind and simply don't go there. You're closing and locking the door to the mental archive. But how about those situations where you aren't looking for sin, but sin is out looking for you? Let's call that level 24. In this battle the insurgents are trickier. An invitation to lust can sneak up and attack you in ways that no actual human being with adulterous copulation on the mind could.

Our culture has many "acceptable" predators. Have you ever been blindsided by a lewd image or suggestion you were not looking for? The fashion industry, entertainment industry, advertising industry, and sex industry know their business well. They are looking to find you, to snag your heart, to shape your identity, your goals, your worries, your spending. Some of my examples arise because we live in a culture of visual media, where such ambushes are increasingly common:

- You're simply watching television or a film, and the plot, language, and action take a suggestive, racy turn. You are being played with.

- You're doing a book search on the Internet, looking for an out-of-print theology book. A slightly mistyped web address pipes hardcore porn onto your screen. Or you open an email that looks legitimate, but it turns out to be well-disguised spam spewing gutter words in bold, colorful print. Or you recognize that an email is spam and delete it, but you can't avoid reading the filth on the subject line. You feel splashed with sewer water. You weren't looking for sin; you didn't linger; but you're dirtied anyway.

- In the grocery store, a handsome, charming young man starts to flirt suggestively with you, a mature, married woman with well over a hundred thousand miles on your odometer! Is there an answering flutter inside you?

- You hear that a certain movie is worth watching, but get blindsided. A lewd scene was gratuitously inserted into an otherwise good movie for the sake of avoiding a G rating. Or the cinematography is beautiful, but deep emotional empathy is created for a man and woman whose respective spouses are portrayed unfavorably. The couple is portrayed as committing wondrously life-affirming adultery. Are you neutral and detached? Disgusted? Somehow hooked?

- You're driving down the highway, and *voilà*, a twenty-by-sixty-foot billboard advertises Coors beer by featuring a lady wearing practically no clothes. Wouldn't it be wonderful if there were nothing inside answering back to her call? If only that ad created the same indifference as the neighboring billboard, on which Citizen's Bank advertises its thrilling new mortgage rate that could shave 0.25 percent off your current rate! Suddenly, you're in a fight you didn't start. You didn't do anything to put yourself in harm's way. Nobody (except God and your conscience) will ever know if you sin by responding to the Coors woman's initiative in a way that commits adultery in your heart. No one ever came under church discipline or was sued for divorce by driving on the interstate and looking twice at a billboard. But that's where the ambush occurs.

You can have a lot of light growing in your life, good latticework in place, gardens of healthy sexuality. But wherever there's still a broken lattice, an oily stain, then an inner spark or inner flinch can answer to what comes at you. Redemption proceeds exactly in such places. You face things that whisper the very messages that once shouted in your life. Yet Christ speaks loud and clear; so at this level, too, you learn to choose well.

Sins So Atmospheric They Seem Like Who You Are

Sometimes lust is so subtle, it doesn't even seem like lust—until you think about it, unmask it, pull it toward the light: level 32. For example, have you ever battled the instinct to size up a person on the basis of sexual attraction? It can be a largely unconscious evaluation. Subliminal radar registers and explores someone on the wavelength of mildly sexualized desire. A quiet current trends in the direction of lust. You're subtly aware of a body's shape, of the cues communicated by posture and gesture, of the messages expressed through clothing, hairstyle, makeup, scent, tone of voice. This subtle attentiveness correlates to the heart's erotic attraction: "Is this person desirable to me, worth further exploratory interest?"

Perhaps this impulse rarely surfaces into conscious awareness. Perhaps you almost as instinctively say no, resisting the urge to steal a lewd look. (Thank God for a garden of light within the lattice! You're given unchosen, unplanned fruit of the Holy Spirit!) But the very atmosphere of such erotic intentionality subtly stains you. It is yet another aspect of your battle with darkness.

When you recognize sin's subtlety, you realize how much your life hangs upon sheer mercy from God. He is utterly aware of thoughts and intentions of which we may be barely aware or wholly unaware. Mercy extends here, too.

Who can discern his errors?
>Declare me innocent from hidden faults.

. . . .

Let . . . the meditation of my heart
>be acceptable in your sight,
>O Lᴏʀᴅ, my rock and my redeemer. (Ps. 19:12, 14)

The stains that corrupt our hearts are not simply the planned, willful, chosen, enacted sins that emerge at the more obvious levels of our battle.

Is it possible to alter the subtle tendencies that pattern how you look at people? Yes. The Holy Spirit is about this business. It takes a while: a lot of walking on the paths of light, a lot of needing God and loving God, a lot of receiving his mercies, a lot of learning to genuinely love people. But you can grow wiser even at this subtlest of levels. You can increasingly view each human being as a sister or brother, a mother or father, a daughter or son—as someone to care for, not a sexual object. Your gaze and intentions can become more and more about caring and protecting.

Levels of Subtlety in Responses to Being Sinned Against

I've chosen examples from the active sins. But there is an analogy for those who have experienced the dark splash of evil as victims of others' treachery, violation, and violence. In some ways, it can be "easier" to deal with an abusive relationship (level 1). Hard as it is to escape, it can be done. The problem is clear cut and definable. As in adultery, the wrongdoer can be caught in the act. Violence can be intercepted. The needed action steps are fairly obvious. Friends will help you. The law can help protect you: police intervention, a restraining order, criminal charges against the offender. You can flee. When you aren't in the same room, the person can't hurt you anymore. There are places to live where you are safe.

But how do you deal with all the residual effects (level 8)? How do you disentangle the effects on health, finances, friendships, family, living arrangement, children? How do you deal with your reactive sins—self-pity, hostility, bitterness, alcohol or drug abuse?

And how do you deal with the memories (level 16)? Memories aren't as bad as being abused, but they can be worse when it comes to getting rid of them. They inhabit the shadows of your mind. They break out unwelcomed, to play and replay scenes from your suffering.

Or, again, how do you deal with the fact that your pump is primed to interpret anyone's irritation at you as a threat of imminent violence (level 24)? You've learned to deeply trust and love your God and a circle of dear friends after torturous experiences many years ago. You've learned not to shrink from new people. Your new boss treats you reasonably well, but his appearance, voice, and mannerisms bear some uncanny resemblances to the person who once betrayed you. Where that person was cruel, your boss is only irritable and sarcastic on occasion. His sins are 1 percent of what you once experienced; but that's where today's battle erupts.

How do you deal with the subtle fears that you now bring to all relationships, apprehensions so automatic that you're not even aware of them (level 32)? These nearly invisible motions of your soul are pervasive, hard to intercept, and highly corrosive to developing future trust and love. Safe refuge, peace, and watchful care run deep in the Psalms. God is trustworthy at every level. Psalm 23 means something very good at level 1, something still richer at level 16, and wonders beyond wonders on up through level 32 and all the way home to level 40. The significance of the Lord's kindness is not exhausted at the more obvious levels. The Psalms go deep, deeper, and deepest the more you bring complex, honest experience to the table.

Truly Changed, Truly Changing, and Still in the Fight

All this—from level 1 to level 40—is the arena of sanctification. Heart, soul, mind, and might are being conformed and transformed into radiant purity. A heightened view of our conflict with sin and misery brings with it a heightened view of the significance of our Redeemer, Jesus Christ. One of the deep truths of sanctification is that you get better and worse at the same time!

You truly shine more brightly as you move toward the light. You hold onto God more steadily. You're more loving and joyful. You're more trustworthy. More teachable. You give to people rather than use them. But brighter light also exposes more dark corners, pockets of unconscionable and once unimaginable iniquity. As we have seen, sin is not only the worst things I ever did. John Calvin captured well the historical wisdom of the church regarding these things:

> The children of God [are] freed through regeneration from
> bondage to sin. Yet . . . there still remains in them a continu-

ing occasion for struggle whereby they may be exercised; and not only be exercised, but also better learn their own weakness. In this matter all writers of sounder judgment agree that there remains in a regenerate man a smoldering cinder of evil, from which desires continually leap forth to allure and spur him to commit sin.[3]

A smoldering cinder of evil, a restless inner motion of sin, says, "I want. I need. I demand." And Jesus's strong mercies and strong call are renewed every morning, saying, "Turn to me for mercy. Repent of your impulses as well as your actions."

Calvin's comment vividly describes the inner battle with active desires that lead to active sins. But there's more going on in the human heart. As we've noted throughout this book, "reactive" fears also quiver within. Clear self-knowledge and seasoned pastoral wisdom carefully probe the difference between desires and fears. The Lord addresses the fainthearted in a very different way than he addresses unruly and lustful desires. When you are gripped with apprehension, or you doubt that your Father could ever love you, or you're confused about how to think and what to do, or you flinch at the memory or possibility of being harmed, he simply says, "I am with you. Do not be afraid. I know what you are facing. I will never leave you or forsake you." Fears, shame, confusion, a sense of abandonment, and painful self-condemnation can continually darken the human heart. Fears are false prophets, breathing threats and prophesying disaster. When fear and trembling seize the soul, the impulse to flee is strong.

> Oh, that I had wings like a dove!
>   I would fly away and be at rest. (Ps. 55:6)

Sin tempts a person to flee into a shell of self-protection or a haze of chemically altered consciousness. But Jesus says, "I am your refuge and strength, a very present help in trouble. Turn to me for safety."

The struggle with our own weakness includes the things that make us quail, that quench awareness of God, that put smoke in our eyes, that discourage our faith. They infuse discouragement, a sense of being dirty and shameful, and a false sense of being guilty for the evils perpetrated against us. In 1 Thessalonians 5:14, Paul describes how ministry deals with unruly hearts, with faint hearts, and with those who are simply weak and overwhelmed. Christ ministers patiently toward all.

The Poor in Spirit, Truly Blessed

The poor in spirit are blessed because the kingdom of heaven is theirs (Matt. 5:3). For all of us, whatever our struggle, Jesus's first beatitude is first for a reason. Awareness of our impoverishment and need for mercies from outside is the opening motion of living faith. Jesus's blessing on the inwardly poor is "first" not in the sense that once we've experienced it, we can move on and leave our need for grace behind. The first beatitude is foundational. It sets the shape and infrastructure of the entire building. The better I know my Christ, the better I know my need for what he alone is and does. The first four beatitudes emphasize our need, dependency, and submission to God. The second four move toward strength, generosity, purity of motive, fruitfulness in helping other people, and courage and joy when life is hard. The Beatitudes map out how you find help in your own struggles and how you become helpful to other strugglers.

When you understand your subtle sinfulness and God's mercies, you will never say of any human being, "How could he do that?" or "She's so unbelievable!" We are fundamentally more alike than different. You have a thoughtful compassion because Christ shows you persistent compassion. You may never have been an adulterer, fornicator, homosexual, or consumer of pornography. But you know with all your heart that no temptation overtakes anyone that is not common to everyone (1 Cor. 10:13).

And when you understand both how horrifying and overwhelming sexual violation is and the necessity of God's mercies, you will never say of any human being, "Why doesn't she get over it?" or "Why is he still struggling?" There are tears not wiped away and fears not entirely soothed until the last day. You may never have experienced a predator as frightening as the one portrayed in Psalm 10. But other people have. And Psalm 10 gives you a sense of how helpless, threatened, crushed, and terrifying a victim can feel in the face of malice. You will know with all your heart how important it is that our Lord will bring

> justice to the fatherless and the oppressed,
>> so that man who is of the earth may strike terror
>> no more. (Ps. 10:18)

And you will know how significant it is that God is faithful.

Grasping the subtlety of the battles helps you to grasp the true depth and scope of the work of our Savior. And you can pray with confidence,

> according to your steadfast love remember me,
> for the sake of your goodness, O LORD! (Ps. 25:7)

8

REMEMBERING THE

GOAL OF RENEWAL

We've looked at many varieties and dynamics of sexual darkness. The Great War with sin and affliction is longer, wider, deeper, and more subtle than we might first realize. The enemies within—desires and fears—fight harder than we might imagine. And it is thus no accident that the height, depth, length, and breadth of the love and work of Jesus are more wonderful than we first perceive. What is God after in remaking our lives? Is his purpose that we would just stop sinning? Is his purpose to get us diligently involved in having quiet time, participating in public worship, finding fellowship? Yes, stop sinning. Yes, use the means of grace. But that's not the goal. The point is to become like Jesus in real life. The purpose of grace is revealed in character and lifestyle: love, humility, trust, courage, and every other good thing.

Jesus starts to rearrange how you work as a person. You

have a qualitative change of heart. You live life in God's direction. He rearranges how you treat people. You have a qualitative change of life purpose and lifestyle. A James Ward rendition of the spiritual "Glory, Glory Hallelujah" puts it this way:

> I won't treat you like I used to,
> since I laid my burden down.

Let me give two simple examples.

Example 1: You Treat Others Properly

First, you learn to see and treat all people in wise, constructive ways. A familial principle sets the norm. In general we are to view and treat all people as if they were beloved sisters or brothers, mothers or fathers, daughters or sons, grandmothers or grandfathers. The line is clear. Anything that sexualizes a familial relationship is wrong. You don't make out with your grandmother or leer at your brother. True affection and fierce protection go hand in hand. The notion of incestuous sexuality is abhorrent before the face of God. That's not just for biological reasons; it's a moral principle. This is the principle operating when Paul encourages Timothy about all his relationships: "Encourage [an older man] as you would a father, younger men as brothers, older women as mothers, younger women as sisters, in all purity" (1 Tim. 5:1–2).

With marriage, a second category comes into play. One person of the opposite sex moves from being strictly familial and becomes your husband or wife. All your sexuality belongs rightly and freely to that person. The notion of a treacherous sexuality—infidelity—is abhorrent before the face of God.

There is one other category of persons to consider, based on how they treat you, not how you treat them. Males and females whose intentions are unfamilial and sexualized are threats to your welfare. They bring darkness. Again, the lines are clear. Nothing about your relationship with them is to be sexualized, so flee temptation and seduction, whether in person or in imagination. The notion of accepting an invitation to consensual immorality—in whatever form—is abhorrent before the face of God.

Love is radically free to be fiercely faithful—properly familial, properly marital, properly wary.

This is not complicated. People frequently seek to blur the lines. Scripture has this to say to us when we are tempted to make sexual immorality blurry: "Let no one deceive you with empty words, for because of these things the wrath of God comes upon the sons of disobedience" (Eph. 5:6). Blurred lines are deceptive, empty, and disobedient. The God of love is the God of life. Sexual immorality is not love, and it brings death.

It is worth reiterating that this makes sexual self-restraint the most normal thing in the world. If you are unmarried, restraint is Christ's norm 100 percent of the time. If you are married, restraint is normal 99 percent of the time with your spouse (and 100 percent during certain seasons). And restraint is normal 100 percent of the time with all other people. Life is not a playground of potential sexual objects.

Example 2: You Treat Good Sex as Normal

A second example of a renewed character and lifestyle is that good sexual love is simply normal. Sometimes the idealized view of good sex can sound overheated, even when we prize and protect marital sexuality. Sometimes we can get the idea that good sex (in both the moral and physical senses) is a gymnastic, ecstatic, romantic, athletic, electric, semi-psychotic, erotic, high-wire, bug-eyed, luxuriating, ravishing bliss of marital passion!

Sorry to disillusion you. But much of good sex is just—well—normal and everyday. Think about it. Most people in the history of the world have lived in one-room huts, where the kids slept in the same room with their parents! Countless families have lived in flats, with only curtains for room dividers, your mother-in-law in the far corner, and your wife's younger brother sleeping on the couch. Or they've lived in tents, as nomads. Not much soundproofing or privacy in that housing arrangement! And not much in the way of gymnastics or sound effects possible if you have children. That's not to say that a married couple with children shouldn't get away for a weekend, or close the door, or do things to make sex special. There's nothing wrong with some high-wire encounters that bring a little extra spice.

It's helpful to think of the analogy with food, another of life's very redeemable pleasures and, unlike sex, a true physical necessity. Occasionally you pull out the stops for a memorable feast with all the fixings: Thanksgiving dinner, for instance. But in normal life, you eat a lot of healthy breakfasts. In the redemption of sex, a lot of normal aspects of a relationship flourish. How about courtesy? Basic kindness and patience? How about humor—pet names, teasing, irony, private jokes? Good sex is not *that* serious! How about mercy? How about a shower, shave, and being relaxed? How about a fundamental willingness to be available to another, simply to give. How about conversation about how each person is doing? How about quiet, slow, leisurely time together? Basic love goes a long way toward making good sex good. Maybe the Richter scale occasionally tops out at an earth-shattering 8.0. But in normalized good sex, you'll also enjoy 3.5 temblors that hardly rattle the teacups.

Get your goals straight. It heightens the significance of your Savior. He alone restores you to practical love for God, to the practical, familial love appropriate for each of your various kinds of neighbors, and to the practical sexual love that is one part of all that is appropriate in marriage. Christ makes everyday life shine with visible glory.

GETTING DOWN TO TODAY'S

SKIRMISH IN THE GREAT WAR

Renewal. I've talked about the war, the direction of the journey, and the destination. The final word in restoring joys to the sexually broken is to get down to business. Our daily renewal has three parts.

Identifying Today's Skirmish

First, *where* is today's skirmish? Your battle always gets fought at the next step, not all at once. "Today's trouble" is where you find God's aid. A clear view of what you face defines your "choice points," the forks in the road before you. Where are you tempted, now? It might be sexual. But remember that the skirmish is not always about sex. God keeps many issues in view as he works out our sanctification. How are you handling life's pressures? Are you complaining or anxious? Does self-righteousness make you defensive and judgmental? Are you working too hard or being lazy and escapist? Are you forgetting God? What's your relationship with money? Whenever you skirmish well in any area, it has ripple effects into every other area of life. For example, Tom had to figure out how to refight his Friday nights so he wouldn't keep coming out a loser. He had to rethink his basic expectations of God, and the way he had misaligned his whole relationship with God.

How about you? Is darkened sexuality even the prime battleground today? And in dealing with what darkens sexuality, what are you dealing with somewhere between levels 1 and 40? Where is today's choice point? The current struggle is the place where the Vinedresser is pruning. It's where you need life support from the Vine. Making all things new is always about something going on today. Restoring pure joys is not theory. It's what's happening here and now. It's not about instant perfection (I hope that's clear by now).

And it's not about yesterday. If you're still brooding and obsessing over yesterday's failures, then *today's* choice point is "How do you handle failure?" Can you quit curving in on yourself after you fall, and begin to deal with your sins by relying on free mercies? You'll always need your Father, Savior, and Comforter to help you, forgive you, and teach you. Today's trouble identifies where.

Finding God in Today's Trouble

Second, what one thing about God in Christ speaks directly into today's trouble? Just as we don't change all at once, so we don't take in all of truth in one massive Bible transfusion. We are simple people. You can't remember ten things at once. Invariably, if you could remember just one vital truth in the moment of trial and then seek your God, you'd be different. Bible verses aren't magic. But God's words are revelations of God from God for our redemption. When you actually remember God, you do not sin. The only way we ever sin is by suppressing God, by forgetting, by tuning out his voice, switching channels, and listening to other voices. When you actually remember, you actually change. In fact, remembering is the first change.

Here's a simple example. God says many times, "I am with you." Those are his exact words. How does taking that to heart utterly change the script of *your* sexual darkness? What if you are facing a temptation to some immorality? For starters, nothing is private; no secrets are possible. "I am with you." "I . . . am . . . with . . . you." Say it ten different ways. Say it back to him, the way Psalm 23:4 does: "You are with me." Slow it down. Speed it up. Say it out loud. You'll probably find that you immediately need to say more: "You are with me. Help me. Make me know that. Have mercy on me. Don't forsake me. I need you. Make me understand."

You will find that the competing, lying, tempting voices become more obvious. They are sly and argumentative. They will try to drown out God's reality. They will scoff at what God says. They will scoff at you. They will seek to allure you or overpower you to plunge you into a dark parallel universe that has no God.

To the degree that you remember that your Lord is with you and you seek him, then those other voices will sound devious, tawdry, and hostile to your welfare. How did they ever sound so appealing? The contrast, the battle of wills, the conflict between good and evil will be more evident. Your immediate choice—which voice will I listen to?—will become stark. Remembering what's true does not chalk up automatic victory. But we do secretive things only when we're kidding ourselves. Every time you remember that you are out in public, then you live an out-in-public life. "I am with you" means you're always out in the open.

Even if you sin by high-handed choice, you will still be in broad daylight before God's searching eyes. He's still here. You can open your eyes, listen, and turn around in order to find help. He who loves you says, "I am with you" to awaken and encourage you.

What if you face a different struggle today? What if you feel overwhelmed with aloneness and fear, buried under your hurt, abandoned and betrayed by people? "I am with you." "I *am* with you." "I am with *you*." Again, when you really hear that and take it to heart, you know you are not alone. You are safe. Someone's manipulative and violent lust violated you; the steadfast love of God never betrays you.

Or what if you're overwhelmed by the grime of past failures? You feel guilty, shameful, unacceptable and ask, "How could God ever accept me?" He responds, "I am with you." God is not shocked by the ugliness of your real-time evils. He came to give his life for the "foremost" sinner (as Paul twice calls himself—1 Tim. 1:15–16). Christ truly forgives. Truly.

Whatever your struggle, "I am with you" changes the terrain

of battle. You start to see the fork in the road. There is a way of life. Your choices count, and you can choose life. A good road runs uphill toward the light, where previously you only knew to stumble over the edge into the abyss.

Talking and Walking with God

Third, put trouble and God together. Start talking and start walking. We already began to do this in the previous paragraphs. It was impossible to identify choice points and to offer promises and revelations of God without starting to capture the honest human responses: faith in God and constructive love for others. Like the Psalms, put trouble and God together and talk it out. To "remember" is not a mechanical recitation of Bible verses. You are seeking help today. That matters—even though you know that tomorrow or next month or next year your battle will mutate into some new form. We are not yet what we shall be, but we are growing toward it, step-by-step in real life.

Walking in the light is not magic. When you can see the fork in the road more clearly (today's skirmish), and when you see and hear your Lord more clearly (something he says), then you start needing, start talking, start trusting. And then you start making the hard, significant, joyous choice to love people today.

Go into action in today's skirmish. That's our final word. It gets us down to where our Savior intervenes to make a difference. It's where our Father is making us more fruitful. It's exactly where the Spirit of life is renewing us into his image of light and delight.

NOTES

Introduction
1. Julian of Norwich, *Revelation of Divine Love* (London: Burns, Oates and Washbourne, 1927), chap. 27.

Chapter 2. Making Renewal Personal
1. Chris Tomlin, "You Are My King," 1998.
2. Augustine, *The Confessions*, trans. Maria Boulding (Hyde Park, NY: New City, 1997), 198 (8.17).

Chapter 3. Renewing All That Darkens Sex
1. William Shakespeare, *King Lear*, act 3, scene 2.
2. Marriage per se is neither magic nor magically loving. The last part of this chapter will discuss sexual sins that can also occur within marriage.
3. The "Peace Prayer of Saint Francis" was published anonymously in 1912 and later attributed to Francis of Assisi when it was printed by a Franciscan priest on the back of an image of Saint Francis, according to Christian Renoux, "The Origin of the Peace Prayer of St. Francis," accessed October 17, 2016, http://www.franciscan-archive.org/francis cana/peace.html.

Chapter 4. Renewal Is Lifelong
1. Martin Luther, "From Depths of Woe" (Psalm 130), 1523; composite translation.
2. John Newton, "Amazing Grace," 1779.
3. John Calvin, *Institutes of the Christian Religion*, ed. John T. McNeill, trans. Ford Lewis Battles (Philadelphia: Westminster, 1960), 3.3.9.
4. Martin Luther, "Defense and Explanation of All the Articles," *Luther's Works*, vol. 32, ed. George Forell and Helmut Lehmann (Philadelphia: Fortress, 1958), 24.

Chapter 5. Renewal Is a Wider Battle

1. This characterization partly arises from tendencies within American Christian culture. Other Christian cultures may do their calculus of the conscience a bit differently. In Uganda, for example, anger is particularly shameful, the bogie-man sin that automatically disqualifies from ministry. But Ugandan Christians often view sexual immorality the way Americans view outbursts of anger or gluttony. Such behaviors are sinful but aren't uniquely shocking and damning.

   Dante's *Divine Comedy* portrays "normal" sexual sins—sensuality, fornication—as meriting a shallower circle in hell. Like gluttony or sloth, these are distortions of normal desires. But sins of treachery, sexual and otherwise, involve betrayal of trust, and those who commit them sit in the deepest pit of hell.

2. Bob Dylan, "When You Gonna Wake Up," 1979.

Chapter 7. Renewal Brings an Increasingly Subtle Struggle

1. Fyodor Dostoevsky, *The Brothers Karamazov: A Novel* (New York: Macmillan, 1922), 108.

2. The video-game metaphor captures a progression of different *kinds* of battles we face. It does not capture how in real life we also "regress" and may have to fight an old battle over again. It also does not capture that in real life the subtler sins are actually present all the way through. But they don't tend to come front and center, while some other struggle is more overt and decisive for that moment.

3. John Calvin, *Institutes of the Christian Religion*, ed. John T. McNeill, trans. Ford Lewis Battles (Philadelphia: Westminster, 1960), 3.3.10.

GENERAL INDEX

SCRIPTURE INDEX

How Does Sanctification Work?

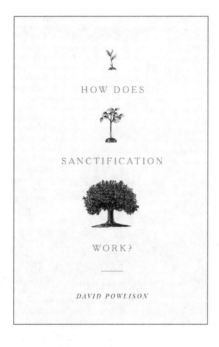

Weaving together personal stories, biblical exposition, and theological reflection, David Powlison shows that the process of sanctification is personal and organic—not a one-size-fits-all formula.

"David's is a voice of sound, biblical wisdom in the midst of much confusion. If you are looking for a book on sanctification that is profoundly personal, biblically balanced, and deeply relevant, then this is it."

Heath Lambert, associate pastor, First Baptist Church of Jacksonville; executive director, Association of Certified Biblical Counselors

For more information, visit crossway.org.

Restoring Christ to Counseling and Counseling to the Church

COUNSELING
ccef.org/counseling

WRITING
ccef.org/resources

TEACHING
ccef.org/courses

EVENTS
ccef.org/events

"CCEF is all about giving hope and help with a 'heart.' If you want to learn how to effectively use God's Word in counseling, this is your resource!"

Joni Eareckson Tada, Founder and CEO, Joni and Friends International Disability Center

"The vision of the centrality of God, the sufficiency of Scripture, and the necessity of sweet spiritual communion with the crucified and living Christ—these impulses that lie behind the CCEF ministries make it easy to commend them to everyone who loves the Church."

John Piper, Founder, desiringGod.org; Chancellor, Bethlehem College & Seminary

Christian Counseling & Educational Foundation
ccef.org